One Camino
...Three Journeys

from Natalia x

One Camino
...Three Journeys

Tricia Fairclough

First published in 2021 by

Escritor Publishing Services
Ferndown, Dorset.

ISBN 978-1-9161933-9-0

Reprinted 2021

Copyright © Tricia Fairclough

Typeset in Sabon by Escritor Design, Bournemouth

Printed and bound by CMP UK Ltd, Great Britain

escritor
PUBLISHING

Acknowledgements

A huge THANKS to all who made this Journey possible...

Friends who, over a four year stretch, variously accompanied me along the stages of the Camino de Santiago as we celebrated retirement and ... 'because it's there'. Kay, Maggi, Monica, Sue, Trish, and Diana, Roger and Bunny.

Ben who kindly gave me advice on Dissociative Amnesia. (purely co-incidental naming of one of the characters).

Writers' Group especially Cynthia and Janet for their advice and support.

Mum, no longer with us, who instilled a love of the written word.

Friends who politely remained interested in this long-winded project.

Likewise Adam, my son.

Finally, Andy, my husband who has shown patience and encouragement throughout and as a final gesture, offered to produce the illustrations.

Sketch map of the Camino, showing
major towns visited en route

Contents

Part 1, St. Jean Pied de Port to Burgos

1

Bryony

'THERE'S NO TURNING back now…' Alone and feeling self-conscious, I stood on the station platform at St Jean Pied de Port. Collapsing my walking poles to put across the top of my red rucksack, I heaved it onto my shoulders then tightened its straps. These unfamiliar actions gave me time to look around, at the same time becoming aware of my pounding heart. I was well out of my comfort zone and boy, what a realisation. I steadied my breathing whilst busily checking my pockets, always a useful tactic when needing to stall the situation. Quite a few like-minded people were engaged in similar activities, many standing alone, some in small groups or in pairs. I noticed that red seemed the predominant rucksack colour, which was reassuring.

My first decision needed to be made – which direction to take to reach the town. There was a sign which, even for the non-Spanish speaker made sense, but I always preferred the animate over the inanimate when having to make a solo decision so hung around waiting to see in which direction my fellow travellers took.

'Probably something to do with age.' My girlfriends and I would lament. 'Signs can get moved round or fade, technology fails and is far too complicated, maps are hard to understand, people … well they just know.'

I watched and waited as the train doors on this local line were banged shut. Apart from other walkers there were a few local people making their way along the platform; schoolchildren with their school bags, women carrying shopping baskets, and some workmen carrying the tools of their trade. Not an English voice to be heard.

Being late summer it was still very warm but cloudy. Beyond the station and through the clouds, the peaks of the Pyrenees created a backdrop of beauty; dark and forbidding on one hand but mystical and inviting on the other. This was it, I had arrived, there was no turning back, at least not without a lot of explanation to those I had left back in my home town....

✦

Friends' reactions had ranged from the amazed to the sceptical when I announced my intention to walk the Camino de Santiago.

'You? Why?' was a frequent question.

Hotly followed by, 'Where?' or 'The Camino? What's that?'

'You'll never do it,' said the sceptics.

'You're mad, mid-life crisis,' joked my close friend, Ellie.

The only person to take me seriously was Jack, my husband of twenty years. My rock, my soulmate, my lover and best friend ... well, all those, until a year ago when our relationship went into free fall following revelations from each of us. We still shared the family home, which had never become a 'Family Home' in the true sense of the phrase, still entertained as if all was well, still had an element of respect for each other based on our shared past life but beneath this veneer of normality our lives had changed irrevocably.

I had initially been drawn, in a superficial way, to the Camino after watching the film The Way starring Michael Sheen. The beauty of Northern Spain, so different from the provincial town close by the village I came from, lodged in my mind. The seed of this idea grew over the months as I borrowed books about the Camino from the library, read up about the different regions the route would pass through, and even found myself pouring over maps of the journey. It was when I found myself attending a talk being given by a member of a church in the next town who had recently returned from the pilgrimage, then searching shop windows for walking boots and rucksacks instead of heeled shoes and handbags, that I realised the seed had become a small fruit which was developing in my mind.

Despite the friction between us, Jack saw how serious I was and encouraged me in my plans. He travelled with his work as Senior Accountant for a large retail business and went on regular golfing holidays with his friends, which I always agreed was an acceptable 'man' thing to do. I had once tried a holiday with Ellie, but it was not a great success. Within the confines of our village, we may have shared grievances over our respective love lives, even our sex lives but the minutia of daily personal life was another matter. Differences, not apparent when we got together at home, manifested themselves under the searing Greek sun. Sunbathing differences, trips out to explore the locality, even whether to have another carafe of wine with our meal caused ripples of dissent. Not to mention the time taken by Ellie each morning in choosing which bikini to wear. As for sharing a bathroom, I still shuddered at the wasted time as Ellie locked herself in and appeared later looking little different from when she had entered. We agreed compatibility did not go beyond days out together.

'Seems mad but I admire you for trying. Go for it.'

That statement made by Jack, and my various friends' ongoing comments, goaded me into serious action. Training became a regular part of my day, reading all about other 'pilgrims' experiences fired my excitement, shopping for all the equipment and clothing gave me a sense of achievement long before I even set off. How different it was to be handling walking boots rather than heeled shoes which I used to buy on a whim, for them to languish with so many other pairs in my 'shoe cupboard'. I had even followed the instructions for wearing them in by taking regular walks in our local woods. I convinced myself at the time I was also wearing in my body and my mind as with no-one to talk to I was learning to 'be happy in my own skin' – a phrase offered by Ellie.

The main reason for my decision to walk the Camino had not been taken lightly. Our revelations to each other about people who had entered our respective lives had been the impetus, but secretly I had been looking for a challenge. I was bored with the life of morning coffees and visits to the gym, of idle chat and meaningless shopping. Much as I loved my friends' company there was something missing. Being an only child with both parents dead I couldn't join in on family chat neither could I brag about children (not for the want of trying!). We had briefly discussed adoption or IVF but neither was pursued. I was lonely in a crowd, lonely at home, lonely even when Jack was in the house.

Then, without warning, the 'someone else' I had confessed about to Jack appeared on the scene, excited me and, more importantly, made me feel like a real woman. He was a Canadian, Paul, here on an exchange at the local university. We had met at the local coffee house, each buried in our own thoughts until I inadvertently trod on his foot as I passed by his table. Sounds ridiculous I know but it's the truth. That first meeting became the first of regular meetings – at different coffee houses, mainly in the next town. Coffee and companionship then became shared secrets and sex. We each knew there was no future, it didn't come up for discussion, he had a partner back home, I had Jack – well we shared our house if nothing else. At this point I hadn't realised our trysts were probably being played out not so far away by Jack and his 'friend'.

Things between Jack and me finally came to a head one evening when, after a few too many drinks, he referred to me as 'Susie' – Susie, for God's sake! Where did she come from? I knew there was a Susie in his office and I probably wouldn't have picked up on it if he hadn't become flustered and exacerbated the whole situation by uttering four short words.

'I'm so sorry Bry …' and the flood gates opened.

His and mine. Revelation after revelation. Shouting, anger, pent up thoughts, mainly petty but obviously itching for release, with separate rooms to follow.

It really was an awful time as we skirted around each other with a restrained politeness. When he went out, I stayed in and vice versa. After a few days we began to unfreeze and admitted to each other how cathartic our respective disclos-

4

ures had been. However, it was also obvious we had deep-rooted problems which at the time neither of us could see a way through, and so our separate lives continued; under the cloak of harmony as far as friends were concerned, neither of us particularly happy but, and that's how our conversations always ended, 'But …'

I was consumed by my preparations to the point where even Paul began to take a back seat. My friends commented on the empty chair when meeting for coffee as I continued focusing on what lay ahead. Truth be told I was becoming nervous and fearful but I had made this commitment and was resolute in my determination to achieve my goal. I tried to push the anxiety to the back of my mind as excuses were made to all.

Jack and I agreed on no final decisions until I had completed this mammoth endeavour, which was how I was beginning to see it, and here I am.

✦

The platform emptied. It was mainly young male and female foreign voices that alerted me to the direction I needed, my first hurdle had been taken.

The cobbled street led to the Pilgrims Office. It was a hive of activity as maps and books were being purchased. I watched as leaflets were being handed out giving lists of hostels. I could deduce discussions about the weather and the organisation of first night arrangements. Amongst the hustle and bustle a voice alerted me, an English voice. I glanced over and saw another girl, maybe slightly younger than me, carrying a navy rucksack, picking out leaflets. It was difficult not to introduce myself but I recalled reading how walking alone allows for self-reflection and personal development and I had made a somewhat tentative vow to journey solo. Evenings would be an exception as to share a meal with others would allow me to expand my understanding of other people and places. Prospective pilgrims from other countries crowded the office but I couldn't help myself gravitating towards the voice.

The girl was asking about hostels and the weather. She supplemented her English with a spattering of Spanish and was making herself understood better than I had so far, even though most of the assistants spoke some English. Her red hair was tied in a ponytail and her facial features were weathered as if outdoor life appealed to her. She had an air of confidence, which at this present moment was still eluding me. It was as if the enormity of what lay ahead was now a reality as I watched and listened to the voices, laughter and in some cases seriousness of those surrounding me. The girl smiled her thanks and left. I lingered over the scallop shells, an important but not compulsory accompaniment carried by many pilgrims as a symbol of the journey ahead, but left without buying one. What had I done so far to deserve it? The significance of the shell was important to all pilgrims but surely it had to be earned? I did however buy a Passport: a booklet to be stamped at each stopover. I had seen pictures of the fascinating stamps and was looking forward to owning one, such meaningful evidence of my journey.

As the office emptied, I realised I was stalling – avoidance tactics, anything to put off the inevitable. I knew I had to make a start otherwise I wouldn't reach my first night's accommodation which I had pre-booked from home. This had been Jack's idea and I was thankful for his concern. The one-star hotel lay over the border in Roncesvalles, some way off. There was a hostel in the monastery grounds but I had decided a room to myself and a good night's sleep was imperative for my physical and mental well-being. I gathered up my rucksack and walking poles and headed down the narrow street and towards the bridge that crossed the River Nive. I stopped to watch the waters gushing beneath. Back home, a bridge was usually accompanied by a game of Pooh Sticks from my *Winnie the Pooh* days with my nephew and niece. Not today though.

The whole town seemed alive with a collective sense of anticipation of the unknown as pilgrims of all ages and nationalities stepped out to overtake me. I turned to take one last look at the comfort of the bustling town and headed off into the unknown; the first of many steps on my journey was made. The sky was clear, the sun not too intense.

'Some pilgrims – of a certain age – take the first part of the first stage by taxi,' I recalled the suggestion offered by Ellie. 'It's really steep to begin with, so the guidebook says anyway. Baptism by fire and all that. There's no point knackering yourself on Day One, struggling up and then over the top of the Pyrenees. According to the book it says ...'

I had been scathing of such an idea and given her short shrift.

'Taxi – you've got to be joking! Start with a taxi? Shall I do it all by taxi then?'

The climb was indeed steep; my cardio vascular system was put to the test and my calf muscles tightened and tensed as I walked, trying to link my breathing to my steps. I gradually found a comfortable pace and moved slowly onwards and upwards. The ferrules on the tips of my poles gave a satisfactory soft thud as I moved my poles in time with my pace.

'Bon Camino', the words spurred me on as other pilgrims passed by.

'Bon Camino,' I replied cheerfully. 'I'm on my way. The Way ...,' I whispered to myself.

As I stopped for a drink and to tighten my rucksack straps, a taxi slowly ground its way past. It stopped ahead of me.

'Can we give you a lift?' A man's head poked out of the window. As I drew level, I saw a couple roughly my age.

'We've decided to make a head start, not only is it bloody steep, it's a long day for day one,' the lady gave by way of explanation. I peered in the window.

'Six more weeks ahead, why wear yourself out on Day One?' she continued. I detected perfect colloquial English spoken with a husky, undeniably French accent.

Her partner nodded in agreement.

'Just because St James – and Shirley Maclaine – did it the hard way, doesn't mean we have to stress ourselves before we've really started.'

Ellie's earlier words of wisdom, what seemed a lifetime ago, and my vehement response came back to me. Already the devil on one shoulder was competing with the angel on other.

Shame to say, the devil won and I climbed in, justifying my decision based on not being in the first flush of youth.

The couple introduced themselves, they were indeed French, recently retired and like me decided they needed a challenge. The pastor of their church had invited his flock to a slide show of his journey following in the footsteps of St Jean along the Camino to Finisterre in order to raise funds for the church roof. They were hooked following his enthusiastic talk and felt compelled to follow in his footsteps, or was that the real reason? Within the first few minutes I discerned a tension between them; not from what was said, more from what wasn't. They reminded me of the last weeks Jack and I spent under the same roof prior to my departure. He was encouraging but cool towards me whilst I was nervous but excited. I introduced myself to the couple (truth be told I've forgotten their names) but decided to remain superficial with my history – basic information only – and allowed their idle chat to pass me by. I concentrated on watching out the window answering questions with economical truth.

The taxi finally bumped over some rough grass and eventually came to a halt. The taxi driver pointed ahead. I knew from my research that the Statue of the Virgin Mary should be close by, the first of many monuments to encourage pilgrims along the Way, and there she was set against an impressive backdrop of the surroundings mountains. Red kites soared and dipped through the clear blue sky. Peace prevailed until a sense of the inevitable took hold as I took my purse from my body belt but the couple refused payment.

'Bon Camino until we meet again.' And they were off, red and blue rucksacks firmly in place, stepping out with a shared timing which implied plenty of past experience. Perhaps I had been too hasty in my earlier judgement but did it matter? No, it didn't. I had far weightier thoughts on my mind.

I spent a little time alone, talking quietly to myself. I smiled as I looked up into Mary's eyes, inanimate but compelling. Was she willing me to succeed? I crossed myself, which was more of an involuntary action, slightly embarrassed I looked around, no-one in sight.

'OK Mary, time for a quick snack before I set off. Forgive me for cheating, I promise I won't again.' I crossed my fingers behind my back; a fluttering within seemed to reinforce the enormity of what lay ahead. I looked into the distance, Red and Blue, as I had decided to call the French couple, could be seen as little dots on the horizon. A tussock of grass was a welcome seat as I tucked into an apple and small bag of raisins brought from home. Lurking in my rucksack was also a packet of slightly dry ham and cheese sandwiches bought the previous day on arrival at Biarritz airport. I decided the cheese was still safely edible but removed the ham just in case. I certainly didn't want to start my journey with an upset tummy. This I washed down with water, my first solo pilgrim meal, it was hardly enough to sustain, but I had accomplished it – I was on my way. Overhead, the red kites continued to whirl and dive, I shaded my eyes from the bright glare of the sun as I followed their pathways, it was as if they were encouraging me to move on.

'Freedom,' I whispered, then cast around to see if others were close by to hear.

'I bet you'll end up talking to yourself.' Ellie's words brought a smile to my face, as did the answer I remember giving.

'Talk to myself? I've been doing that for years.'

I studied the early pages of the Camino guide, checked my bearings and for some reason thought about the essentials needed on a daily basis. The words were like a gentle chastisement; a reminder that organising daily food rations is as important as having dry socks. I looked at the screwed up empty food bag, then at my watch. Without thinking I pulled my mobile from my rucksack, hesitated, then returned it and stood up.

'Get a grip,' I shouted into the wind. 'You can, you will, do it. One foot in front of the other.'

My pace quickened as I used my walking poles to keep the rhythm going and with the wind in my back the kilometres passed.

'Day One: aim for the first albergue over the Spanish border.' Wise words offered by a friend of a friend what seemed so many weeks ago. It was important to concentrate on the way ahead, not to feel guilty for ignoring nature; that would come as the Walk eased. I allowed for water stops only, once to wash down a headache pill. My earlier confidence began to waver as the climb upwards continued to remain tough. My calves ached, my back felt sore where my backpack was rubbing – something to investigate when I reached my first overnight stop – and I reluctantly decided I wasn't going to reach Roncesvalles today. There was no point in pushing myself to my limit.

From the map in my guidebook I knew there was an albergue close by and backtracked to find it. What a culture shock! They had a bed, or should I say a bottom bunk in a dormitory for six (first time for everything). Clean but basic came to mind, I was in at the deep end. I did feel a warm glow as my passport was stamped, and allowed myself the luxury of sitting on the decking in the warmth of the late afternoon sun. As I sat, I realised I had not given much thought to Jack or Paul, or anyone back home. I now idly wondered if Jack was using the meals I had left in the freezer, or was he otherwise engaged anywhere else? I had told him one of the points of the walk was to go solo and to that end would not be constantly in touch, but I felt he was entitled to know all was well and so a quick text served that purpose.

After a solitary but satisfying supper in their restaurant I turned in early, deciding if I could get off to sleep the top bunk occupant might not disturb me. Luckily, I awoke early to find no-one in occupation, in fact there were only two other occupants of the dormitory, both still asleep. I quietly investigated the straps on my backpack, loosening them slightly. The night's sleep had worked wonders and I was keen to get going in order to reach Roncesvalles by the end of my second day. I bought some provisions from the lady managing the hostel and set off, full of enthusiasm for the day ahead. Acquiring food had not entered my head so I was thankful for her thoughtfulness as I mentally made a note to remember to buy snacks when I had the opportunity.

The climb did not seem so arduous and my spirits were high. I allowed a brief stop to touch the border stone as France became Spain. Other pilgrims greeted me cheerily but in the main my voice remained within my head.

I was walking through a wood of beech trees, the sun dappling through the branches, when a sudden panting behind me grew louder. No-one had passed for what seemed an age and this noise disturbed the air, similar to the sound of an animal seeking a path through the undergrowth. I gripped my poles tightly as I looked over my shoulder to see a young man, red of face and damp of hair; his running pace barely slowed as he approached. I drew into the side of the track to allow him to pass, he finally stopped but kept running where he stood.

'Bon Camino, Kathleen.' A broad Irish accent accompanied by a wide grin. He ran on the spot for a few seconds, just sufficient for me to take in a shock of dark curly hair, deep smiling eyes and a lean body.

'I think you have the wrong per–' I realised these were the first words I had uttered to another person in some while but I wasn't given time to complete my sentence.

'Can't stop. Where're you heading? You on your own?' Questions were fired at me like bullets from a gun. Then he stopped, rocking backwards and forwards on his feet giving me long enough to answer. More questions: was I really on my own? (not sure what he meant by that so gave the answer I thought he wanted to hear.) Am I happy? God knows where that came from but it unsettled me; a loaded question if ever there was one. I sensed he was hoping I might engage further but I refrained from doing so. I did not like this personal approach from a stranger so wished him Bon Camino. He didn't appear affronted by my lack of communication.

'Until we meet again,' and he was gone. All I noticed was Marilyn Monroe's red lips on the back of his T-shirt.

I sat for a few minutes, nearly falling backwards as I did so. The rucksack on my back was a reminder to sit and stand with care. I gulped back water, nibbled on the bocadillo bought from the hostel and tossed a few sultanas down my throat. Eating gave me time to assimilate the short conversation. 'Happy' is such a subjective word, a word of the moment. Yes, I was currently happy, I felt at peace with the world but deep down, unresolved problems existed. Jack? (definitely) Paul? (possibly) My future? (absolutely). All serious in their own right but I had only just begun this journey and had more important issues to concentrate on.

I shivered as I sensed a coolness in the air. The sun was beginning to weaken as I emerged from the woods and on to a stony track. Loose scree made for difficult grip as I used the poles to support me. The track went downhill and up again disappearing into the distance. Empty fields with scant wire fencing but no sign of habitation. No hamlet, no village, no sign of life. I felt very alone and had to remind myself this was part of my plan. My pace slowed as the sound of my phone deep within my rucksack gave its own familiar ring. A moment's hesitation but strength of mind overcame emotional desire to respond to the unknown caller; I had passed the first test. Ahead, faint lights heralding the end of Day One pierced the gloom of early evening. The final push down towards Roncesvalles was hard, my legs ached and weariness enveloped me but achievement was the overriding sensation.

I found a room in the small hotel I had previously booked, it was basic but clean, allowing me overnight privacy. I could not face dormitory sharing on a regular basis as I remember telling my friends. This was one thing I was not prepared to compromise on when options were available. The room looked out over the road which allowed me to get my bearings.

Youngsters in shorts, sandals with T-shirts proclaiming slogans, some as weird and wacky as others were serious and making a point. They were all heading in the same direction leading to a large building, which turned out to be an ancient monastery complex set back amongst trees across the road. I could feel my shoulders thanking me as I removed my backpack; my posture improved immediately as I stood tummy in, shoulders back, rotating them in their sockets forward and back. My whole body relaxed as I removed my boots and peeled off my damp socks. Not a blister in sight! My training had paid off, well for Day Two anyway. I did a few leg stretches to work on my calf muscles which were feeling tight and heavy then unpacked my rucksack and lay everything on the bed. A quick shower and into a pair of decent trousers and a long-sleeved shirt, smart but comfortable.

My next challenge then had to be overcome. Where to eat? I wasn't used to solitary dining, in fact don't think I have ever sat in a bar, cafe or restaurant by myself, apart from waiting for a friend or family member. This was a steep learning curve I was putting myself through but hey, others did it and so could I! The camera lens on the back of my phone drew me towards it. I turned the phone over, two texts: Jack, and Jack again. I left the phone lying on my bed, grabbed my purse and went downstairs to follow a small group of older pilgrims.

'Ola,' I smiled as I caught up with them.

'Ola, bonjour.' One of them smiled at me then resumed the conversation he was having with a companion.

I fell in behind them as they entered what appeared to be a large refectory next to the monastery. Circular scrubbed wooden tables filled the room, each laid for eight people. The place looked as if it should have been lit by candles but the holders fixed to the walls were all electric. A buzz of conversation in many languages filled the room. I stood alone, one hand in my pocket, looking around for the possibility of a familiar face, which was daft considering my whereabouts.

'Ola,' an elderly gentleman with a long white beard stood alongside me. With open toes sandals giving air to no doubt weary feet, crumpled trousers and shirt and rumpled hair, he looked like any other pilgrim.

'We are all pilgrims from many countries so we do not ask from where, just ... welcome.' His English was perfect.

'Follow me, please.'

I became the eighth person at the table, my fellow companions smiled and welcomed me with friendly greetings. All ages, all nationalities, all seemingly sharing a common bond – the Camino. Before there was time for introductions a bell rang, a simple prayer was offered up and the clatter of dishes began. A steaming casserole was placed in the centre of the table, with a basket of bread accompanying it. The elderly gentleman appeared at my elbow with a carafe of wine and a water jug.

'Feel free to leave a donation for the meal on your way out.' His charismatic smile took in the whole table. 'For many of you this is rather like the First Supper! May you experience many more on your journey.'

For the first time since I had left home, I felt a pinprick of emotion. I suddenly realised the magnitude of the journey that lay ahead and the potential ramifications of the decisions to be made regarding my future, and Jack's of course. I had accomplished Days One and Two, I was still in one piece and up until now hadn't time to miss anyone back home.

'Hi everyone, my name is Daisy.'

An English voice brought me back to my surroundings. The girl from St Jean. Before I had time to respond another joined in until all had volunteered their names: an American – or was it a Canadian accent, two Japanese guys, two German men and one female with an accent I couldn't quite discern, possibly Eastern European. Karl from Germany poured the wine and Daisy the girl from England passed the casserole to her neighbour. It smelt delicious and we all agreed the walk had made us ravenous. Conversation flowed; we were all sharing a common experience and each had a tale to tell.

'How about you, Bryony?'

Before I answered I looked around the refectory taking in the camaraderie being shared, the sounds, the smell, the flickering lights.

'I don't think I've ever spent a whole day wrapped in my own thoughts with no-one else to think about ...' I hesitated as if deliberating on my next words. 'I did speak briefly to a French couple and had an exchange, well half an exchange, with a young man from Ireland.' I proceeded to elaborate on the Kathleen incident. 'I wondered whether he might be here but I can't see him. He's probably halfway to Santiago already.'

The others agreed this was a sight to watch for and I felt quietly satisfied I had broken the ice on my first shared pilgrim meal.

The evening passed all too quickly as superficial chat took over. We all agreed we would be starting out at different times in the morning but would keep an eye out for each other along the way. I felt more confident to face tomorrow knowing I had now engaged with others; we were all sharing the same experience, hardships and good times alike. The two Japanese offered their excuses which broke the bond of companionship. People were starting to drift out, I looked at my watch and realised how weary I felt.

'Are you staying in the hostel?' Daisy had come to join me.

'No, I decided if I was to complete this challenge I've set myself I was going to need a good night's sleep each night. All my research about hostel life and how this walk is an opportunity for good; how it would encourage me to throw off the comforts of everyday life etc, etc, convinced me I still needed a little comfort – in the form of a room to myself and a bed, not a bunk. I 'hostelled' last night, not a real word but I'm sure you know what I mean. It was OK, mainly because it was quiet but it reinforced my decision. Did I see you in St Jean, in the Pilgrim Office? Yesterday?'

Daisy grinned. ' Probably, I was there, picking up some leaflets. It was very busy wasn't it? Good for you for starting out basic, I'm hostelling tonight but I did promise myself the luxury of a hotel every now and then … when the going gets tough. Hostels might give me a greater chance of …' she stopped in her tracks as if choosing her words carefully, '… meeting others.'

I sensed there was more behind Daisy's words but said nothing. She fished some euros out of her pocket and placed them in the large shell receptacle on a table in the entrance hall.

'Maybe we'll bump into each other along the way?' It was more of a question than a statement. She sounded confident, as if she was on a mission, which of course she and all of us were. I deliberately gave a non-committal answer as a way of strengthening my resolve to succeed alone. It reminded me of my earlier meeting with the French couple – being pulled in two directions – but this time I stuck to my guns. Daisy put her head light around her head. As she switched it on it temporarily blinded me.

'Whoops, sorry, need to get the hang of this. Good night then.'

She followed others making their way towards an extension to the monastery. I suddenly realised I had arrived with insufficient time to explore my surroundings. I had read about it in my guidebook but not seen it for myself. I wasn't a great history enthusiast but I vowed to at least walk around it in the morning before I set off and reminded myself I should aim to arrive at my destination each evening with sufficient time to explore, however superficially. I didn't want to reach Santiago with no experience of places passed through.

I lay on my bed back in my room and watched a tiny cobweb fluttering on the ceiling. All was quiet as my mind wandered. What was Jack doing? What would I be doing if I was at home? I looked at my watch; it was only 9.30pm. By now the evening bottle of wine would have been half finished and I would have been sleepily transfixed to the small screen, or in our case, the rather large screen, 'All the better to watch sport on,' was a favourite remark of Jack's. As this memory came to mind, I saw him lying on the sofa cheering on his favourite football team. I started to feel emotional and quickly reminded myself that more often than not these days he wasn't lying on the sofa, he was out, elsewhere.

My phone and diary, both on the well-worn bedside locker, drew my attention. I kicked my legs over the side of the bed, fished in my rucksack for a pen and opened the diary ...

I woke with a start, still dressed and no words written. I took off my trousers and shirt and climbed beneath the duvet, turned out the light and exhaustion took over.

✦

I awoke to voices beneath my window. I groaned as my aching legs reminded me of the day before, maybe I should have done a few more exercises on arrival, something Paul had suggested was important. His name brought me up with a start. Was it him who had tried to ring last evening? Or was it Jack? Temptation overtook as I switched my phone back on … it was Jack. The devil hovered but I did not succumb, a flutter within me communicated a developing strength of character. This journey was something I had to do for myself and I would talk when I was good and ready. I idly wondered whether the other girl, Daisy, had set off; beneath her supposed confidence I sensed a sadness within her, secrets held back. How many other pilgrims carried secrets? Probably most of us, truth be told. Would I meet Daisy again? I realised I had been a little curt last night but hopefully there would be an occasion when we might meet, sit and talk. Thoughts of all these people – known and unknown – reinforced a strength within me. We were all alone on our journeys but I suspect most had a past buried deep.

Half an hour later I was on the road, rucksack comfortably settled on my back, water bottle easily accessible, non-perishable snacks purchased and stored away. I reminded myself that tonight proper leg stretching exercises and diary writing were paramount. Tonight? Where would I be tonight? The enormity of the whole experience continued to reveal itself, this was for real, no turning back, no-one to keep me going. I was on my own and I'm not ashamed to admit I suddenly shed a tear. I seemed to be wavering between confidence and vulnerability.

'Self-pity?' It's OK to wallow for a minute, then get on with solving the situation.' Paul's words of wisdom came to mind as I felt in the front rucksack pocket for the little book of Buddhist quotations he had given me. If I never saw him again, which I acknowledged would be quite likely, his last act was one of thoughtfulness towards me. A 'farewell gift' as he had put it.

Having looked at my guidebook I had promised myself a proper stop at Burgos, which was roughly 230 kilometres away. Pamplona, famed for its bull run, appealed but I didn't feel I could justify an extended stop so soon after commencing the journey. I then suddenly realised I had forgotten to walk around Roncesvalles before I left and mentally reminded myself of my earlier vow to at least walk around at each destination.

I was pleased with my progress. I was walking about twenty to twenty-five kilometres each day, (my training back home had averaged seven miles each way from our house, around the common, through the woods, stopping for coffee at a tearoom and back, so my pace was very satisfying). I found inexpensive accommodation each night and to my surprise enjoyed eating alone. It gave me time to think, to people-watch, to speculate. Pamplona came and went. It was a beautiful medieval town where I enjoyed an overnight stay but Burgos was where I was headed.

The landscape varied from busy roads to tranquil wheat fields; from serried rows of vines to shaded woods of oak and ash; from snoozing cats lying in the sun to hustle and bustle of town life. Each brought with it a sense of achievement, a realisation of my developing strength of character and an inner peace. Jack and Paul became memories to unpack at night when all was quiet, think about then pack away. By day, I strode ever onwards with villages coming and going. I stayed one night in Viana, a small town with a market square and side streets cordoned off for its annual bull run the following day. Anything to do with bulls is way out of my comfort zone but a little part of me was curious. The place was heaving with tourists, pilgrims and locals alike and I had difficulty finding accommodation. It was not easy to make myself understood, even though I was sporting all the paraphernalia of a pilgrim, but in the end, I found a room above a cafe, clean but very basic, being just off the market it was also very noisy and to be honest was not one of my better stays. I had a déjà vu moment when I thought I saw the English girl, Daisy, who I had spoken to at Roncesvalles but when I looked again she had disappeared in the throng and I decided I must have been imagining things.

As a city, Logroño disappointed me, it was so noisy, vehicles as well as pedestrians. I felt like I was back home being lured by the fashions in the shop windows and abundant eateries. I decided to ignore its history and after a night's sleep in a decent hotel, moved on. I did have a mini blip at this point, it was as if a modern town reminded me of all I had left behind. Jack, Paul, Ellie, other friends. Jack and I had agreed I would phone him when I was ready. And I marvelled at my ability to carry a phone but not use it. I was surprised to realise just how at ease I was becoming with my own company and I wondered whether this was how Shirley McLaine felt. I had enjoyed her book and, along with Michael Sheen, it was partly her personal, spiritual quest which had sowed the seed even if her reflections were beyond my understanding. I agree I was experiencing a liberation of mind, at least I think that is what was happening, but visions of the cosmos and Atlantis had so far eluded me!

My guidebook was becoming my ever-present companion as details of distances, climbs, villages, refreshing rivers, hostels and hotels drew me onwards. I enjoyed savouring the spiritual quotes, 'A journey of a thousand miles begins with a single step' became my mantra, whilst the practical details prepared me physically for each day and the 'mystical path' reminded me of journeys undertaken in days long gone.

Stopping one night in the Parador de Santo Domingo was one of the indulgences I had promised myself before I left and it did not disappoint. A former twelfth-century hospital originally built to take in pilgrims on their way to Santiago, I was drawn to its rustic but regal interior. A leisurely meal in the restaurant sated my physical hunger whilst the surroundings satisfied my need for a touch of luxury. Spain's forward thinking around converting historical buildings into luxury hotels impressed me. After dinner, the warmth of the evening drew me outside to wander the labyrinth of streets and alleys, taking in the sights and sounds, not to mention the smells of outdoor baking – and in places, drains! But it all added to the charm of the city. To my shame I paid scant attention to the cathedral, vowing to make amends on reaching Burgos. Instead, I found myself thinking that if Daisy from Roncesvalles were to stop here and were we to meet up again, no doubt she would fill me in; she seemed the type of girl to mix culture with walking. As if by way of punishment and despite the luxury of my room, I did not sleep well, probably because of the regular chiming of the cathedral bells.

However, I awoke to a bright morning, refreshed and eager to get started. A slight rub under my left foot warned me to apply a blister plaster and I was on my way.

I was now ten days into the journey and from my guide estimated this to be roughly one quarter of the whole journey. I felt comfortable with the thought of reaching Burgos, maybe spend a couple of days there. Visit the cathedral to make up for bypassing Santo Domingo. Wander the medieval streets, the river park ... just entitling myself to stop and watch the world go by, rest my body, and maybe see a familiar face. I might even break my silence with home.

By now I felt I deserved the right to carry the shell and sought out a shop selling the ubiquitous Camino gifts. As I fixed the shell onto my rucksack, I experienced a tangible shift in my mindset. I was a solo walker, coping – no, enjoying my own company, the experience, the journey, and even the physical pain had its place.

'No gain without pain' came to mind. How true.

My step was strong as I joined a couple of Irish girls, gaily dressed in colourful shorts, tops and headbands. They welcomed my company and we chatted easily. It was their first pilgrimage. 'Because it's here,' seemed as good a reason as any. I mentioned meeting Patrick – the young Irishman – and they burst out laughing as the older of the two, Grainne, explained how he had fancied her friend when they met him a few days past. He had been drinking and gave them a sob story about his past.

'Trying to get us to feel sorry for him.' It obviously didn't work!

We walked together following another small group ahead. The track curved as it followed the perimeter of a field. The group suddenly deviated from the spirit of the Walk and St James's footsteps, and decided to take a shortcut across the field. We followed, albeit I did feel a twinge of guilt. It was tough going underfoot and the wheat scratched at our bare legs – penance perhaps! The heavy soil was lumpy and ridges were unseen.

It was halfway through the field that my day changed for the worse. Despite having applied the blister plaster, I now felt soreness beneath my left big toe and I started to walk awkwardly to lessen the pressure. The ground was uneven and I stepped clumsily, going over on my right foot, I felt excruciating pain in my ankle as I fell forward, landing heavily. I let out a string of swear words, much to the amusement of the two girls. They removed my rucksack and I rolled onto my side, from there they helped me into a sitting position as I wiped away a tear of self-pity and embarrassment; forty something females don't cry in public, do they?

Continued walking was out of the question. Grainne noticed a minor road beyond the track and from the guidebook we knew a village lay beyond. She offered to go in search of a taxi to get me to Belorado, the next town, where I would be able to get medical treatment.

It didn't take too long for her to return with an obliging taxi driver and I bade farewell to the two girls. We said we would look out for each other in Burgos but from past farewells I knew this was a comment made lightly; funnily enough I hoped if anything Daisy might be the one I would meet. Belorado was a small town and the pharmacy was closed. The thumping pain in my swollen ankle was demanding attention so, again, Burgos was where I wanted to be, regardless of the cost.

The taxi driver was very obliging but spoke little English. He nodded when I pointed to Burgos on my guide map. I took two paracetamols from a packet and as I did so my hand and phone connected. I looked at my watch: 11.08am – Jack would probably be on the golf course and Paul, where might he be? Lecturing? Having a coffee in our favourite coffee shop? On the phone to his wife? In the supermarket? I realised I had no idea where he might be. What did this say about our relationship? What was it based upon? Companionship? Sex? Excitement? All three? Now was not the time to dwell on the where's and what's? My eyes drooped, my concentration wavered, I swigged the pills down with water, relaxed and closed my eyes.

An hour or so later, l had been dropped near a pharmacy and soon after that my ankle had been attended to. With a promise to rest it for at least forty-eight hours I limped towards the nearest bar close by the cathedral. I ordered a cerveza and weighed up my situation. I needed to find a room, have a shower and rest. The kind waitress pointed out a nearby small hotel which had spare rooms, they were basic but clean and tidy. It was lovely to lie out on a bed and I drifted off to sleep having now checked my phone (no messages).

I awoke to a rumbling tummy. I needed to eat as close by as possible. With my ankle still aching and heavily strapped, walking any distance was out of the question which was frustrating as this had been my planned proper stop. It wasn't now a case of the tug between the devil and an angel it was a pull between annoyance with myself for the fall and acceptance of an enforced rest. I took some pain killers and returned to the bar close by the cathedral, rested my foot on an empty chair and ordered a tortilla and another cerveza, mentally noting my slight shift in drink choice from my usual white wine or G&T to beers and ciders. The cathedral, with its Gothic architecture (I had done some homework!), towered above me as I took in the surrounding medieval streets alive with weary pilgrims, camera snapping tourists and locals going about their everyday tasks. I relaxed in the warmth of the early afternoon sun and allowed the atmosphere to wash over me as the pain killers took effect.

Two or three days here seemed very appealing and would give time for my ankle to heal and an opportunity to gently explore. An early night beckoned; decisions could be made in the morning.

I lay on my bed listening to the sounds below my window. Laughter, earnest, conversations, voluble tourists all mixed in a cauldron of voices. I felt distanced but not alone. I switched on my phone – low battery. Only time for a quick call home and Jack obviously came to mind, he deserved an update. If I was him, I would be getting worried. My phone battery would not allow for two calls as I then briefly thought of Paul. First decision made; Paul was history. I scrolled down to the P names, found his surname, co-incidentally starting with P... DELETE – from my life. I rang the home phone, then Jack's mobile. No answer from either. I wasn't so much worried, more annoyed. Where was he? Who was he with?

2

Daisy

I ADJUSTED MY headlamp as I left the albergue in the village of Cirauqui. Four days from St Jean Pied de Port with just over a hundred kilometres covered so far and physically I was in good shape, which surprised and heartened me. This time last week back in the comfort of home I was a nervous wreck as I made final preparations for this mammoth undertaking – to find Ben. Here I was now, looking forward in more senses than one as another strenuous day lay ahead. I was a world away from friends and family and well out of my comfort zone but my focus was resolute.

Today was forecast to be continued warm weather (as I heard from two pilgrims 'breakfasting' by the side of the track) which heartened me. Cirauqui had been the first of many medieval hilltop settlements along the Camino and I had spent the previous evening exploring its narrow, winding streets. Having read about its ancient houses bearing armorial crests, much of my time here had been spent looking up at the coats of arms depicting flowers, animals and unrecognisable carvings over the solid wood panelled front doors. Spending time wondering about the history that lay behind these antiquities temporarily took my mind off the reason for my being here, which in turn relaxed me and allowed me to recharge my mental and physical batteries.

Ahead, tiny pin pricks of light from other early risers flickered in the shadows of dawn. I felt reassured to know there were others already on the road but annoyed with myself I had again not engaged meaningfully with any fellow pilgrims. Four days and nights as a solitary walker, meals taken alone, apart from sharing a table with seven others on Day One at the hostel in Roncesvalles. I had enjoyed that meal; it had set me up for what lay ahead, made me realise I need never be truly alone. The girl sitting across from me – Bryony from the UK – came to mind, she sounded quite an extrovert, probably good company, but like me had not completely indicated her reason for the Walk nor had she suggested a need to walk with another. I casually hoped I might bump into her again. Was this a subconscious reason? A need to engage with someone from home? I dismissed these thoughts; there would always be others along the Way, each with their own reasons and desires, with whom I could engage should I so wish.

Even though I felt quite confident in my solitary walking, the whole reason for my being here and the one thing I had still not done was raise the opportunity to talk about Ben, my missing son, Ben. I was annoyed with myself that I was finding it difficult to broach the subject whether to passing pilgrims or those who, like me, had stopped for the night somewhere. Despite him being uppermost in my mind I could not fathom why I was less than confident to broach the subject of his disappearance, but I reassured myself there would be many other opportunities, as much of the Camino lay ahead with many others tramping its path.

Again, it had been a restless night, what with the girl on the top bunk snoring, and others in the dormitory shifting and turning and muttering in their sleep. During the course of my research and reading of accounts written by so many who had gone before me, I had read and mentally prepared myself for adult communal sleeping facilities but what was written did not match up to reality and to say I felt jaded was an understatement.

'You, sleeping with others, you'll give that idea up after Day One, I bet.' I recalled the words offered laughingly by my friends at the farewell evening they had arranged for me. Champagne had flowed, the meal was superb.

'Your Last Supper,' someone had said, much to the amusement of all present. I laughed along with them but inside me the Last Supper was churning.

'How are you going to cope bunk sharing?'

'Is it true dormitories are mixed?'

Questions I light-heartedly threw off were now coming back to haunt me. Last night it had been an all-female dormitory but that did not necessarily mean the next ones would be and male snoring well … the less said about that the better. I felt in my rucksack – dark navy like Ben's – for a piece of chewing gum and my hand made contact with a plastic folder I had pushed down one side. Inside was a photo of a lean, suntanned young man, a dog-eared postcard of the magnificent medieval city of Burgos, still many kilometres away, some small A5 posters and my guidebook. I also felt the rough cover of my still virgin notebook, which guiltily reminded me I had already broken one promise to my friends, to write an entry every day.

✦

My friends from our village meant everything to me since my somewhat small family had contracted from three, to two and now me, alone. They were there at times of past despair, they were there to keep my fridge full, my house tidy and my mind intact. They made sure I went to the hairdresser regularly (my red, wavy hair was my pride and joy) and took it in turns to treat me to a pamper session. My parents were marvellous, they did what they could, but so often I, with my grief, was the one supporting them with theirs. They had aged physically and mentally whilst I had shrunk physically and mentally but I had always tried to remain strong for them. The disappearance of Ben was, for them, the loss of their only grandson. Ben's father, Shaun, no longer part of our life – now living abroad with his new wife and family – had returned to the UK and, in fairness to him, was a great help in liaising with the authorities who had entered our lives literally overnight. Ben, then aged twenty-one, had set off to walk the Camino on the adventure of his life and his disappearance was the reason for this huge empty void in my life. My boss, and owner of the estate agency, had been generous of spirit to allow me unpaid leave.

'Take as long as you need, just bring that lad of yours home.'

I always sensed my boss had a soft spot for Ben after he had undertaken work experience when he was at secondary school. He is polite and respectful, if I say it myself, and perfectly capable of laying on the charm when needs be, just like his dad was.

*

As I walked, the shell I had bought from the Pilgrims Office in St Jean Pied de Port, hung down from one of rucksack straps, gently swaying in time with my steps, and my water bottle was secure in the webbed pocket. My sun hat was firmly on my head even though the sun had so far refused to appear. To be honest, it was the cloudier days which made for easier walking especially as I was walking through open farmland. A few stern words of encouragement and I was ready for what now lay ahead in my search along the Camino. I had now already covered 135 blister-free kilometres and apart from aching shoulders and calf muscles I felt physically fine. A tiny bit of self-congratulation wafted in and out of my thoughts quickly to be replaced with notes of caution as many more days of solid walking lay ahead. This was my Walk, my mission – proof, if needed, of my desire to move forward with my life, in more than one sense of the word. In searching for Ben no stone was to be left unturned; if necessary, I would trip over each one and delve beneath its surface.

The going was good underfoot as the sun finally rose over the wheat fields to my left. From the mental and physical agony of my first few days had emerged a walking routine; when to stop, when to change my socks, when to treat myself to an added break. I had established that vistas were to be treasured and wayside bars acknowledged. From the map, the terrain further ahead looked reasonable, in fact it looked inviting, it was just the landscape to recharge my batteries. Oak and beech woods, a quarry, beautiful countryside with walnut and olive groves and just a handful of smallish villages and towns that would punctuate my Walk and, more importantly, would be filled with other walkers of whom questions could be asked.

It pleased me that I was the one saying 'Bon Camino' as I strode onwards. My rough-hewn walking stick was my constant companion.

*

Some years ago when Ben, as a young child and I set off on a walking holiday in the Lake District, my father had surprised us just as we were about to leave. Never one to engage in complicated practical skills, he had produced two walking sticks lovingly carved from a beech tree. Mine had a star carved into the handle.

'Look up at the stars and see their beauty, and in that beauty see yourself.' (A quote by Draya Mooney. I loved the quote even if I didn't particularly rate her and her American B list celebrity style).

Ben's walking stick was shorter and its handle had two small ears carved into it.

'Listen to me, son,' my father used to say when a man-to-man chat was required, to which Ben would reply, ''Ere we go again,' and they would laugh together.

I smiled as I remembered how Ben would hold the handle in the palm of his hand with his fingers wrapped around the ears. 'Comfort feeling,' he would say.

Both Mum and Dad had engraved their names and a simple message. 'We will be with you both every step of the Way.' A momentary pang of sadness pounded in my chest as I recalled the words. Ben's stick still hung in my living room where I could see it every day. His grandfather had made another adult stick for him; a telescopic stick, like a walking pole but made from oak with metal fixings, a stick now missing, along with Ben. Mine too was a gift from my dad, similar to the one he had given Ben so long ago.

It was two years ago that Ben had decided to walk the Camino de Santiago along with a friend, to raise money for their friend whose life had been cruelly cut short. How ironic it was that his walking companion had then been struck down with a debilitating virus resulting in Ben choosing to go 'solo' as he called it. Three friends; one dead, one virtually house bound and one disappeared. I recalled the last time I saw him as we accompanied him to the airport, him with his walking stick and dark navy backpack and me with a sense of pride at what he was about to do. Where is the justice in life?

My journey along the Way was to follow in Ben's steps – wherever they had taken him – with one aim: to find him. My friends had tried so hard to prepare me for disappointment but I refused to accept their cautionary words. I had never admitted to anyone, including myself, that he might just not be found. In these past few days however, with time alone I became aware of a tiny shift in expectation. From 'He is still alive; I will find him' I found myself thinking about the chance he might not be found but that questions asked by me along the Way would provide answers. Whatever the outcome it will shape my future, I will accept and I will move on. Closure in one form or another.

✶

The map in my guidebook showed a tiny hamlet eight kilometres into the day's walk. Beyond that by a short stretch was a small bar which offered rolls and drinks. I followed the path through a wood to emerge onto an ancient stone bridge crossing a lazily-flowing stream. The path took me into the hamlet which looked more deserted than inhabited. Half derelict barns and cottages were scattered and the only sign of life was the ubiquitous plastic bag containing rolls, baguettes or bread hanging from gates or stone walls. The baker's van had already passed through the hamlet. I idly wondered how long a bag of delivered bread would remain on a gate post back home. It was easy to find the bar as I noticed one of two pilgrims emerge from what I had presumed to be a solitary cottage.

'Ola,' they smiled and I returned their greeting. They seemed in a hurry so my opportunity for conversation passed. I lay my stick against the wall, removed my rucksack and entered into the welcome cool of the front room, which seem to double as a shop. I ordered a baguette with ham and cheese, making an effort to use the few Spanish words I had conquered, and chose two ugly, plump, beef tomatoes with dry earth still clogged to them.

'I bet you wouldn't choose those if you were in a supermarket back home.'

I turned to see a young man behind me. An Irish lilt caused a slight flutter as I passed the time of day with this pilgrim. I loved and hated the Irish accent in equal measures. Shaun, Ben's father, was from Donegal and the lilt reminded me of good times but also of great loss.

I took my lunch and sat with my back against a tumble-down moss-covered stone wall which encircled a derelict, stone barn. Across the track in front of me lay a vista of fields, some with sheep but mostly empty. A few derelict stone huts punctuated the landscape as I shaded my eyes and gazed into the distance. I loosened my laces, shook out my socks, applied a Compeed plaster to what might have been the early signs of a blister under my big toe, and tucked into my pilgrim lunch.

'Teitos.'

That Irish brogue hardly had time to interrupt my wanderings as a body slumped itself next to me, a rucksack carelessly strewn alongside.

'I beg your pardon?'

'In an emergency I've slept in one. Cheap, quiet, uncomfortable and something to tell the grand kids ... not that I've got any ... obviously!'

I turned to see a pair of green Irish eyes staring into mine. A huge smile lit up his face as he held out his hand.

'Bon Journo Kathleen, I'm Patrick.'

'That's not my name,' I started blustering and then realised the joke was on me. I suddenly recalled what the girl from the UK –Bryony – had said about meeting a young Irish lad when we ate together at Roncesvalles.

'Can't go wrong with a Kathleen. Bit like me being a Patrick.'

'I'm Daisy, preferable to Kathleen, I once had a great Aunt Kathleen.' I shook his hand.

We sat in companionable silence allowing the distant bleating of sheep to permeate the heat haze.

'I met a girl who you might have spoken to, heading towards Roncesvalles, she said you called her Kathleen too?' I spoke casually.

'Indeed you might have. I made a bit of a fool of myself. I'm running this, well, as much as my legs will allow and my alcohol intake! Excess alcohol last night and I left my wallet in the hostel. Had to go back, then met some old mates and my journey came to a grinding halt. I'm a bit all over the place. Still, plenty of time, nothing else. Lesson learnt.'

He spoke in short, clipped sentences which seemed to reflect his whole demeanour. Staccato, nervy even, which seemed at odds with his easy-going approach.

We chatted amiably mainly about the journey; it was his second time round; he'd been here two years ago but gave no more details. My heart quickened when he said, 'two years.' Ben was here two years ago, but I didn't pursue it. We seemed to be skirting around anything that might draw attention to ourselves. Just as he started to get up, I remembered the postcard and leaflets. I had to ask him, it was the year Ben went missing and I couldn't miss the opportunity. I fished in my rucksack trying to calm my nerves.

'If you've been here before you might recognise this person. The photo was taken in that summer.' I ignored the familiar churning feeling in my stomach as I handed the leaflet to him without removing it from the plastic wallet.

He studied the photo through the plastic. Ben's face, Ben's open smile, his nonchalant stance as he stood for the camera, leaning on the stick carved by my father, as he prepared for his solo journey.

'No, I don't. Sorry.' No more than that. No interest and no questions.

'He is ... well ... was .... No ... is ... my son. He was here, on this Walk. Two years ago. He must have got this far, he must have reached Burgos, look, I have a postcard ....'

I showed him the postcard with a few scribbled words on the reverse in Ben's handwriting:

Reached Burgos. All good.

'I am sorry but I can't help you. Doesn't look familiar.'

He got to his feet and hoisted his rucksack onto his shoulders.

'Adieu Kathleen. Until we meet again. I'm a bit of a bad penny so keep an eye out.' And he was gone, running on the soles of his feet like a graceful gazelle with Marilyn Monroe staring back at me.

Although I was disappointed at what I perceived to be his lack of interest, he had given me the impetus to pursue the reason for my being here. I promised myself – and Ben – I would be more questioning of other fellow pilgrims as I moved along the Way.

My eyes met Ben's. It was if he was looking right at me, smiling at me. I took the photo from the wallet and kissed it. As I did so, Patrick's words came back to me: 'I'm sorry, I can't help you.'

It was a stilted reply. Not surely how one would answer a question such as I had asked. Did he mean that he could but that he wasn't going to? Or he wasn't able to? Or was my imagination running away with me? Was he so disinterested? Lacking in sympathy? If so, why? I sat, trying to regulate my breathing and out of control thought processes.

At that point I noticed a wallet where he had been seated. He'd done it again.

✦

I had reported Ben missing after two weeks of no communication. Then came the worst message any mother could receive. He was dead, body in a hospital morgue, diagnosed sudden teenage heart attack. The Spanish Police were marvellous, met us at the airport, arranged accommodation, nothing was too much. I had flown out with Shaun; I remember that flight as if it was yesterday. We were united in grief and a shared past but both living inside our respective heads with our respective feelings of loss. What is even more vivid was the mortuary, sterile with bright overhead lights with respectful attendants in the background. The faultless attention and sympathy from the hospital staff, and then the discovery – it was not Ben lying there shrouded in white. Same build, similar looking, but it was not Ben. It was Ben's wallet the police had found and used for identification purposes, it was Ben's watch on the body but where was Ben's passport and personal belongings? Despite an investigation by the police and despite, some months later, one of Ben's friends with Shaun searching again along the Camino, nothing revealed itself to us. The worst two years of my life followed as I tried to make sense of how a seemingly healthy, happy, boy can walk out of the door in one country and disappear without trace in another.

*

I looked at my watch, three more hours before I reached my overnight stop. As I walked, I cast my mind back to yesterday's meeting with the young Irish lad, Patrick. He was so friendly when we first met but I sensed there was more to him than he was prepared to offer but was it anything to do with Ben? With so much going on in my head I had neglected to engage with my surroundings but today a feeling of calm accompanied me. The track was easy underfoot as I made my way past tranquil farmland that stretched ahead. At one point my path took me over an N road which reminded me that civilisation was never far away. At another, a feeling of panic washed over me as I realised I had not booked anywhere for the night and I needed to get a move on before all beds were taken. Physically my pace, my breathing and my energy levels were high, less so my mental state. This was the first time I had mentioned Ben to anyone on the journey and memories flooded my mind. I knew I was physically prepared but now realised emotionally I wasn't. It was fine when walking; it was the stopping that engaged the memory. Luckily, plenty of walking lay ahead and my silent promise to find Ben spurred me on.

The hill town of Viana loomed ahead. I had walked about

twenty kilometres and the hills, whilst not the highest on the Walk, had tested me. I was grateful the climb up to the village was achievable without too much exertion. I was looking forward to a shower and a bed for the night. I had decided to treat myself to a hotel, however modest, to enjoy a quiet night away from anonymous snoring and other bodily noises!

I hadn't bargained for it being festival time with a bull run the following day. The village was overflowing with pilgrims and visitors, all rooms taken. In desperation I enquired at a smoke-hazed bar. I felt conspicuous by being female and alone and very obviously not local, but my initiative was rewarded as I was led next door by the owner. His mother owned the house, she could put me up for the night. Gratefully I accepted and we waited whilst he attacked a huge brass knocker on the solid front door. An elderly wizened lady dressed in black from head to foot opened the door and I was left with her in a dark, furniture filled entrance hall. A cat lay asleep on an armchair. My eyes adjusted to the lack of light as I was led along a short corridor. The room I was offered was tiny, it appeared to be unused but was filled with assorted furniture plus a bed pushed in under the window. She offered a few words in Spanish, which I did not understand, and left. I couldn't blame anyone for making a few extra euros on the side but did feel a little uncomfortable surrounded by random objects to step over and around. I loosened my boots and stretched out on the bed.

It was dusk when I awoke, stiff and sticky. I sought out a shower, which was not much cleaner than the ones I had used in some of the hostels, but reminded myself I was not here on a luxury holiday. I took my diary from my rucksack and placed it on a lace covered occasional table. Following my meeting with Patrick, I now had something worthwhile to report alongside other daily events and descriptions. It was good to change into a fresh pair of trousers and polo shirt and my feet felt the better for the airing away from walking boots. Suitably dressed and with my trusty walking stick, I set off to find a place to eat. I also needed to find the local albergue in the hopes my photo of Ben might trigger a memory and that they might agree to pin up one of my leaflets in the reception area.

A nearby notice gave details for tomorrow's bull run – as much as I could understand – so I made a mental note to leave early to avoid getting caught up in the melee. It sounded fun and no doubt very atmospheric but I felt sorry thinking about the bulls who must be scared and frightened (or am I being anthropomorphic?).

I found a busy cafe, one where anonymity could cloak me. Despite my earlier rest, I still felt physically exhausted and past the stage for eating much. I just wanted a snack and then a good night's sleep, so sat at a vacant table by the window and simply ordered tapas and a cider. The service was good as was the food but without company it wasn't long before I had paid and made my way out and into the throng.

As I stood getting my bearings, a familiar face suddenly appeared within the crowd: Bryony, from Roncesvalles. I'm sure it was her, the girl with whom amongst others I had shared a table. I wanted to call out but for some unfathomable reason drew back then inwardly cursed when next I looked as there was no sign of her. I gave myself a stern talking to, my reluctance to engage with others or make the first move was most unlike me. Back home I would quite happily initiate conversation, sometimes to the embarrassment to my friends. Was this reluctance subconsciously steering me away from possible disappointment? Or was this the inward-looking person I had become since Ben's disappearance? Whatever the answer, Ben deserved better. Why else had I spent so long preparing myself for this journey? At the very least Bryony's presence reminded me I had to seek out the albergue. I paid my bill and pushed through the packed streets until I found the ruins of the thirteenth-century church of St Pedro where, my guidebook told me, the albergue was to be found. The ruins drew me in but I resolved to speak with today's people not ghosts from the past.

I leaned my stick against the wall, as others had done before, and entered the hostel. It was an old stone house sitting in the grounds of the church. It was cool after the heat of the day but I could imagine it being cold and cheerless in the colder months. Voices came from all directions, mostly foreign but the odd English word broke through.

I showed the picture of Ben to the girl at the reception.

'Well, he does look vaguely familiar, I think … but obviously so many pass through these doors. I could be wrong. Call back later when it'll be quieter but make sure it's before ten o'clock. I'll have had time to speak to the other volunteers by then. I'm Rene by the way.'

I could hardly believe what the volunteer was saying as I handed her one of my A5 leaflets. An American with a midwest drawl, she explained she had been volunteering in Viana for three years. She did not dismiss me out of hand and, more importantly, Ben was possibly remembered by someone who was not going to deny all knowledge of him, as I still thought Patrick had done.

I wandered the town soaking up the atmosphere. There was insufficient time to explore seriously as my legs ached and my body was crying out for rest, my early night was disappearing into the darkness but with good reason. I would keep my promise for a proper stop when I reached Burgos. The guidebook had already drawn me to its history and beauty and I was very keen to visit its cathedral. More importantly, it would be my last link with Ben.

I walked past the church dedicated to Santa Maria and returned to the albergue office where I was introduced to Señora Rosa Martinez. The room doubled as a reception area and the walls were covered with maps, weather forecasts and photos. Leaflets in labelled boxes filled the shelves along the walls. A box of assorted clothing lay against a wall, clothing left by pilgrims for others to use. This walk was not only about testing oneself it was also about thinking and caring for others. She was kindness personified as she offered me a café con leche and proceeded to study the leaflet of my lovely, handsome son. At one point I found myself holding my breath as assorted emotions coursed through me. My mouth was dry, my shoulders were hunched. The American girl, Rene, joined us, placing the coffee in front of me.

'I shall translate for Rosa.' She spoke gently as she sat alongside and briefly touched my arm as if in commiseration.

She translated as Rosa spoke.

'Like me, she thinks she remembers him but for different reasons. She saw a bit of her own son in him, how he bit his lip when concentrating on one of the maps on the wall.'

She pointed behind me as Rosa continued. It sounded as if she was stumbling over words as her excited hands swept the air in front of her but Rene understood everything.

'She thinks he spent more than one night here. If it was him, he was suffering with a bad cold and fever.'

Tears began to fall, why wasn't I with him in his hour of need? Why had he not contacted me? Is this something to do with his disappearance?

Suddenly, Señora Martinez produced a leather-bound register.

'All guests register their name and country of origin; we then stamp their Camino Passport. Some are eager to shower and relax, others stop by for a chat. I think your son wanted to chat. He and his friends ...' As she spoke, she turned back.

'His friends? What friends?' I sat up fixing her with me eyes.

'I think ... he was with a girl. I can't remember exactly.'

Rene continued translating.

'She was Spanish but spoke some English. Rosa thinks there might have been another boy with them but if there was, he didn't stay here. Neither did the girl according to the register, which is strange as she thought they were together.'

'What else? Did he get better? What did he tell you?' It was my turn to stumble over my words. I handed her another leaflet.

'Are you sure? This is him.'

Rosa took the poster, studied it and placed it with the one I had left with Rene.

'I'm sorry, it looks like him but I can't be sure.'

Rene finished the translating and put her arm around me.

'He must have got better. There's no record of us giving him the doctor's number. Not all hostels keep these records but señora does, she says pilgrims are her responsibility whilst they are staying here.'

'You say the girl was Spanish but spoke some English. Can you remember any more ... or the boy who you think was with them?'

Rene shook her head. Something stirred in my memory. The lad I had spoken to earlier, Patrick, who denied all knowledge, a young man with an Irish accent who had walked the Camino at about the same time as Ben, the year he went missing, coincidence or not?

I gave Rene my mobile number and she promised to contact me should Señora Martinez recall anything further. She hugged me and wished me well.

I returned to my room, my mind buzzing.

I sat on the only chair, a hard backed one with wicker missing from its back. I opened my diary and scribbled and scribbled. I took out my mobile and went to phone Mum and Dad but changed my mind. I promised I would phone if I had anything to tell them. This was not enough; I didn't want to raise their hopes. My eyes felt heavy. I wearily undressed, visited a shared bathroom across the corridor and before I knew it, I was awoken by the sound of a street cleaning vehicle with an orange rotating light which lit up the room. There was nothing for it but to make an early start.

It was good weather for walking, cool with high clouds and the promise of sun later. There were few of us on the road. The landscape was less interesting to begin with and I found my mind wandering back to yesterday's conversations. Ben was ever present and over the next couple of days I made good progress as I talked to him, explaining the journey and my resolve to find him.

It was then that I realised I may have had Ben walking with me but where was my walking stick so lovingly carved by Dad? I racked my brains trying to picture it as I had covered the past kilometres. I was sure I'd had it in Viana, had left it outside the albergue but then what? Where? That was a bad day for me; no Ben, no stick. I gave myself a stern talking to and turned the negative into a positive by thinking how it might be found and help another pilgrim worse off than me. I had lost my stick, I had to get over it and eventually I did. For the first time, a lightness of step drew me onwards as I headed for Santo Domingo de la Calzada. I had noticed from my guidebook that there was a parador on the site of the original pilgrim hospital and decided to treat myself to a night in medieval splendour.

As the day wore on, the landscape mellowed into fertile fields and oak groves. Vineyards abounded groaning under the weight of plumptious red grapes, I picked a few and popped them into my mouth allowing their juice to trickle down my chin, they were delicious. The weather being as it was the grape pickers would soon be busy toiling from dawn to dusk.

I had my wallet with Ben's photo and the leaflets towards the top of my rucksack for ease of removal, but other pilgrims were either on bikes or heads down as they passed me by with a scarce 'Bon Camino'. I was not offended; indeed, my own demeanour had hardly been approachable in the early part of the Walk.

Santo Domingo did not disappoint. The parador was opposite the cathedral and following a relaxing bath I headed out with my plastic wallet in my day bag. I showed Ben's picture to various people but shaking of heads and 'No, sorry' were returned to me in various languages which did nothing to help my earlier positivity. I sat in the cathedral and spoke quietly to any unseen presence that cared to be listening. An overwhelming desire to hear a sympathetic, familiar voice overcame me and I decided to phone my parents that evening. As I sat, I read about Santo Domingo and his devotion to early pilgrims. Thanks to him a bridge was built over the River Oja just outside the village, also a hospital where shelter and aid could be offered and a small church. Today's pilgrims, including me, have much to thank him for.

A sudden sound of chirping hens alerted me. I recalled reading in my guidebook the story behind the chickens in Santo Domingo's cathedral but with so much going on in my head the actual story eluded me. I followed the sound and came across a chicken coop housing a white hen and white rooster. An information sheet told all. Apparently, they were part of a flock kept by the brothers and lived in the cathedral with a weekly change over. The story has it that in days gone by a miracle occurred, saving the life of a young man who was about to be put to death. The myth relates how an innkeeper's daughter fell in love with the young man who was on the pilgrimage with his parents. He spurned her and in revenge she stole a silver goblet and placed it in his backpack. Upon its discovery he was found guilty of theft and sentenced to death by hanging. I continued reading, amazed that even back in those days the course of true love never runs smooth. A short while later, whilst visiting his body, his parents found he was still alive.

Distraught, his parents appealed to the magistrate who was in the process of cutting up two chickens. His response was that their son could no more be alive than the chicken in front of him, whereupon St Domingo carried out a miracle by bringing the hens back to life! The magistrate fell to his knees in prayer and asked for clemency for the boy, thereby saving his life. From that day onwards, two chickens reputed to be from the original flock have lived within the cathedral. I later overheard a guide telling a group that if you found a white feather in the cathedral it will guarantee a successful completion of the pilgrimage. The word 'successful' rung in my ears. I don't believe in miracles but....

I approached the guide as the group wandered the cathedral. I showed him Ben's photo but in return came another shake of the head. Fleetingly I began to question whether Ben had actually trod this path, the postcard showed Burgos but had he been there? Had he indeed passed through any of the villages en route? What had he been doing?

The events of the day caught up with me and I decided I needed an early night. I briefly bowed my head at the altar and on turning to leave, a white feather caught my eye. I still don't believe in miracles but ... today that feather is still on my dressing table.

The cathedral bell chimed as I climbed into bed. A lightness of body and spirit overcame me, any negativity ebbed as my head hit the soft down pillow. Its contents were not lost on me!

That night I slept as I hadn't done for months. It might have been my luxurious surroundings but on the other hand maybe miracles can happen.

Following my luxurious parador night, I set off with a spring in my step and the white feather tucked in the plastic wallet lying against Ben's photo. I thanked St Domingo as I crossed the bridge. Overhead, wispy clouds floated across the sky; a perfect day for walking. Less villages but more wheat fields lay on this part of the Camino, a sea of yellow stretching ahead. Only sixty-five kilometres to Burgos; three days at the most. I became more confident to stop and speak to other pilgrims, to show Ben's photo but there were no more positive responses. I took heart from my overnight stays in Viana and Santo Domingo and still believed that Ben was here, somewhere. Not having made the call home I was now keen to phone mum and dad but challenged myself to wait until Burgos, I knew everyone would be waiting anxiously and the medieval city seemed the ideal place from which to phone.

The three days of walking took me up the Montes de Oca, through delightfully shaded oak and pine woods, and offered me a night in basic accommodation in the beautiful village of Atapuerca. The hostel manager allowed me to pin up a leaflet on the information board, my reasoning being any returnee pilgrims might have their memory jogged. The following morning, I cheated and caught a bus from the bustling outskirts into the city. I had read about the entry into Burgos being more of a hike as it passed through industrialised sites and residential suburbs and I was not alone in my decision judging by other pilgrims waiting at the bus stop!

Next stop Burgos city centre.

3

Patrick

I DON'T KNOW whether it was the silence that awoke me or the light streaming through the high windows. I lay for a few seconds trying to gather my thoughts. The mattress felt hard beneath me and my body was constricted by my partially unzipped sleeping bag twisting about my body. Obviously, another restless night! One sock-clad foot rubbed against the skin of the other and my shorts were gathered around my lower body trapping my bits and chafing at my waist. I gingerly lifted my head to identify the weight bearing down on me; it was my rucksack with contents spilling everywhere. At that point I observed I was lying on a top bunk which in turn triggered my first question of the day; how the feck did I get up here and where is 'here'? Before coming to any conclusions as to my whereabouts, realisation dawned that the silence was caused by the fact I was alone in this dormitory. I looked around the room, other mattresses on other bunk beds lay scattered whilst bits of litter were strewn across the floor. There was a strong smell of stale bodies mixed with deodorant which caused nausea to rise in my throat.

I closed my eyes to try and form a picture. Through a dizzy haze, memories of yesterday and last night slowly became moving images. Meeting another traveller, female, older, no name that I can remember, apart from one I offered to her: Kathleen. Why did I do that? Was that a déjà vu meeting? Didn't I do the same with another female before her? Oh, muddled thoughts, too much to cope with so early in my waking hours ... Didn't she offer me a photo of her missing son – Ben? The same Ben, possibly, who had been my some-time mate from two years back. Did I, like Peter, deny to her all knowledge of him? Doing the walk with him back along then. God, what a time we had until ... Too much to concentrate on now. Then fast forward, last night, a bar in the village, a group of us, different nationalities, different languages, laughter, insults, all trying to outdo each other. Bottles strewn everywhere; spillages sticky on the tables. Camino mates to the core. Each of us on the Walk; each with a reason known only to ourselves. My arm draped around the neck of – someone, who must have guided me here to the hostel. Did they also push me up onto this top bunk? Did they stay the night here? Did they leave without waking me? Who indeed had been my drinking partner?

'Señor.' A voice interrupted my train of thought. 'Señor, diez minutos.' I opened my eyes to see a large woman standing looking up at me. Her flowery apron hung loose and she was holding a mop and bucket. Folds of skin flapped beneath her chin whilst hairy warts on one cheek wobbled as she spoke. I closed my eyes again.

'Diez minutos,' she repeated stridently, as she leaned the mop against the bunk and held up ten fingers.

'Out. Go.'

I looked at my watch. Christ! Eight thirty. No wonder it was silent, everyone else would have been long gone.

'Si Senora.' I responded, trying to look and sound apologetic. It can't be much fun clearing up after a load of overnighting guys who, if they're anything like me, allow personal hygiene to play second fiddle to living it up at a village bar after a day's hard slog.

I half slithered, half fell to the floor, my shorts slipped down to my knees as I noticed they were undone. My rucksack followed, contents everywhere. Luckily, I was travelling light this time so following a quick gathering of possessions I was nearly ready to get out of her hair. I ignored the tutting as I rearranged my shorts, located my wash bag and made gingerly for the washroom. My head was protesting and by

46

default so was the rest of my body. A wet floor, cold water, slithers of abandoned soap greeted me. I decided I would find a water fountain en route.

On packing my rucksack, I then discovered to my horror, my wallet was nowhere to be found. Every pocket, every compartment, under the bunks, tangled within my sleeping bag I searched, to no avail. I sat on the bottom bunk ignoring flowery apron as she deliberately mopped around me muttering into her folds of skin. I racked my brain, unsuccessfully, it was having trouble enough trying to focus on the here and now. I continued sitting until the mop made contact with my foot. I looked up; she was not going anywhere.

Nothing for it, I was going to have to retrace rather than move on. I apologised to her, slung my rucksack over sore shoulders and walked outside to face the day. It was indeed a grand one as a clear sky greeted me. It was an awesome place for the hostel, which was in fact an old, deconsecrated church conversion. Gently sloping hills stretched out in front of me with serried rows of climbing vines. If you think I possess an eloquent turn of phrase you are correct. My upbringing may have been crap but it didn't stop me loving language and by default, poetry. I also loved the outdoors. Put the two together and hey presto you've got a creative appreciator of the landscape!

I made my way to the village; the first bar was still shuttered, the second had signs of life as the owner put out tables and chairs.

I racked my brains for some Spanish to help me. I knew dinero was money, wallet? I had no idea, neither did I know what credit card was.

'Buenos dias señor er ... mi dinero e car ... wallet?' I stuttered my question whilst wildly signing taking something from the pocket of my shorts. He shook his head and carried on opening the graffiti covered shutters and setting out on the pavement boxes of vegetable and fruit. If he recognised me from last night, he gave no indication. Nausea began to rise in my stomach as realisation of my plight took hold mixed with an excess of alcohol. I began to wretch violently and quickly rushed for the alley behind the bar. I bent double, oblivious to the picture I must have portrayed or the sound I was making.

Exhausted, I lay on the ground breathing deeply trying hard to relax my stomach and my pounding head. The sound of a bus alerted me. If my wallet was not to be found in this hamlet, I was going to have to retrace yesterday's footsteps. I had stopped at lunchtime in the previous village, might I have mislaid it there? I hauled myself to my feet and made for the Piazza where the bus was waiting. It was going in the right direction; at least something was in my favour. Luckily I had a few euros in my pocket which I was able to offer to the driver and found an empty seat towards the back. I placed my rucksack alongside and closed my eyes. I was drifting off when a sudden voice and a prodding of my shoulder made me look up ... I swear I was looking up at the hostel cleaner's sister. A dumpy woman in floral apron with hairy warts on her face looked down at me, wrinkling her nose as she eyed me up and down. Reluctantly, I moved my rucksack and equally reluctantly she sat alongside me. Luckily the journey was short, as the movement of the bus was not serving me well.

I stood by the roadside to get my bearings. Being a small village, this did not take long and I set off in the direction of the first bar I recognised. No luck. I was starting to feel seriously worried which did not help the churning still dominating my stomach. My money, my cards, a couple of hastily scrawled phone numbers; basically, the wherewithal to continue my journey. I followed the path alongside a field towards a rural shop where I knew I had stopped. Events were being triggered again, lunch yesterday, Daisy, that was her name. We had sat outside and chatted. She was older than me, did I chat her up? Surely not? I remember she had a really cool walking stick but details surrounding it were vague.

I sat outside the shop and took a slug from my water bottle trying to make sense of our meeting. The cogs in my brain suddenly started to turn faster and my heart responded accordingly. Jesus! Bloody Hell! It was all coming back – it was Ben's ma. A picture of him shoved under my nose, denial on my part, despair in her voice, guilt tapping on my shoulder as I listened to her story – a story I had full knowledge of, a story of regret and shame. We had parted, had I said more? I just could not remember. I did remember there followed a sleep in the sun before heading to a bar to begin an afternoon of yet more drinking, anything to obliterate the afternoon.

'Ah, Señor. It is you.'

A voice penetrated the gloom of the shop. My eyes adjusted to the light, or should I say lack of light. Everything was the same but everything was different. I was different, my circumstances were different, the thoughts in my head were different from yesterday's thoughts.

'Billetera?' The shop owner came towards me waving something in his hand, in his other was balanced a small crate of tomatoes. He threw the wallet in my direction and placed the crate outside the door where other boxes of apples, cucumbers, lettuces and various other home-grown produce were displayed.

'Señor. Gracias, gracias.' I caught the wallet, stumbling over my words as I did so. 'Donde ... er ... est ... where?'

'The kind señora ... you talk ...' He pointed to where yesterday Kathleen – or whatever her name was – and I had been seated.

The least I could now do was buy something as a thank you. The inevitable table and chair in the sun indicated a welcome to stop to eat and drink. A cafe negro and a bocadillo with jambon seemed a good way to start the day. My body was in rebellion mood where beer was concerned. Placing my newly found wallet on the table, I noticed a piece of folded paper amongst the euros. As I unfolded it Ben's face appeared, eyes looking straight towards me. I stared back as a feeling of guilt washed over me. Meeting his mum resurrected old memories and unresolved issues. This in turn then triggered feelings of guilt at the thought of who had paid for my drinks last night. I was unlikely to ever know the answer. God, what a shitty mess I am.

Physically I'm still in good shape, although God knows how, the way I abuse my body. Inside and out. Blister plasters are doing the trick this time round and the elasticated bandage has helped with my buggered knee. But within, plasters cannot heal the turmoil. Emotions of guilt, shame, embarrassment, hurt … I could go on.

Travelling the Camino this time (no guidebook; I reckon I'm the best guide needed) I have deliberately chosen different places for overnight stops.

✦

One maxim I carry through life is to never make comparisons. I spent too much time doing that as I was growing up; schools, houses – never to be called homes. Mum's crocodile of boyfriends who entered through the front door to depart soon after through the back, as far as my memory serves. Their treatment of me lays buried deep, like a stone that has sunk to the bottom of a pond to be covered by weeds.

Superficial friendships which usually went hand in hand with our next move would temporarily ease my loneliness; other friends' homes bore no resemblance to the furnished flats on which Mum frequently took a short-term tenancy, only to move as unpaid rent became an issue. You might ask how I as a young boy knew so much about Mum and her nomadic way of life. Well, not only did she wear her heart on her sleeve spilling the beans to me every time a new man failed to live up to her already quite low expectations, so were her troubles laid bare; missed rent, non-payment of the electricity, not to mention us having to hide when the loan sharks came knocking.

I cringe with embarrassment when thinking about the boy down the road in County Antrim (our fourth move in as many years) with whom I struck up a friendship. I used to love visiting his place, it was warm and cosy compared to our chilly flat. They had a hot meal each evening and watched the TV afterwards sitting on the sofa in their sitting room. His mum was kind, took me in and fed me on many an occasion. The occasion when I stayed overnight and wet the bed in my sleep, my shame in the morning when I discovered damp sheets and how I left without saying anything. We moved on soon after that and my friendship with Peter – as with so many other young kids – ceased to be.

I finally moved out when I was sixteen and left school with no GCSEs to my name. My last school did me no favours. I arrived when they were in the middle of the GCSE course, the teachers were not interested in me or my nomadic record nor I in them. I found work as a labourer and moved into a bedsit. Gran was the only stable part to my life but her health was poor as a result of earlier drink abuse brought about by treatment at the hands of an abusive ex-husband. Basically, my family was – is – Crap with a capital C. Dysfunctional with a capital D. Even my dad did me no favours – or maybe he did - by being one of the 'back door Johnnies' as Gran called them. Mum never referred to him and I never asked, there seemed to be no reason, if he's not there so well and good … up until recently. Gran happened to let slip something about a male friend Mum had years ago who she really liked but as with the others got the back door treatment. What Gran said made me look in the mirror. Dark curly hair, swarthy complexion, jet black eyes, like him if I remember rightly. As a young teenager rebelling against life in our small town, I used to think I looked more like one of the Romanies who travelled around Ireland selling heather and fortune telling. Not to us though, as I reckon they knew it was not worth wasting their time knocking at our door, but Gran had suggested this bloke might have come from Spain. So, was she hinting something to me? I wanted to ask Mum but by then our relationship was shit.

One day, when I called on Mum and got no reply (although our relationship was crap there still existed this invisible and tenuous thread between us and surprisingly, she always sent – via gran – a key to her latest move for me), I let myself in and for whatever reason found myself in her bedroom, not somewhere I would normally choose to visit. I knew she had a box of stuff under her bed but hadn't a clue what was inside and for the first time ever curiosity got the better of me. It turned out to have a boring collection of brooches that I suppose meant something to her, also her birth certificate. I remember sitting on the floor trying to read it by holding it towards the window in the dark and dreary room. I remember that awful feeling you get in your stomach when something comes out of the blue and hits you in your solar plexus: the address of a mother and baby home in Galway, no mention of a father just my mum's name in the infant's column and Gran's name as the mother, aged eighteen. So, Gran's errant husband had not been Mum's father, or had he? So many secrets, so many lies. I didn't and still don't know who all these fathers are; my mum's or mine. History had then repeated itself as far as Mum was concerned. I remember feeling gutted that a birth certificate in my name was not amongst the contents of the box so I still don't know whether I'm of Romany or Spanish stock, if indeed either.

When I told Gran what I had discovered she was remorseful but no more forthcoming and for some reason suggested I talk to Father Dickinson, and that is how my first Camino journey came about. In hindsight, I think she was at her wit's end where I was concerned and hoped he might set me back on the straight and narrow.

Gran had been more of a mother to me than her own daughter and her words will stay with me always.

'Go your own way, a stor' At first I had no idea what she meant, but a friend explained it meant 'my treasure' which really touched me. I can't say I actually checked whether he was right or not, I just like to believe gran loved me enough to say that. She eventually sat me down and gave me a few more 'snippets', as she called them. She thought my dad had once lived in northern Spain, said he was tall and lean (so am I), that he came from a strict Catholic family but had rebelled at an early age (a family trait there!), was fit and ran a lot (same as me). With so many coincidences, my emotions, which I usually kept suppressed, came to the surface. Who was this man? Did he know I existed? Mum was on another of her benders or she was out of my life at that time, I can't remember which, so kept my conversation with Gran to myself.

That was how I found myself two years ago drinking dry the bars of Northern Spain on a haphazard search for my dad. I ended up along the Camino de Santiago, which seemed a strange choice of journey for a lad such as myself but there it was waiting for me, all thanks to Father Dickinson. I wasn't looking for spiritual redemption but certainly imbibed it on a far too regular basis.

Father D (as he allowed me to call him) was OK, he was kind and non-judgmental. I used to go round to his place sometimes when the going got tough and because of him, two years ago ... here I am again.

That first journey along the Camino yielded nothing, not that I searched seriously, but what a time I had, making and breaking friendships, footloose and fancy-free, answerable to no-one but myself. I can't say I was disappointed at not finding my dad but I made some good mates and, more importantly, it gave me time for reflection on my past and thoughts for my future. Which is why I knew I would succeed at the long-distance walk again this time round having trained as an Outdoor Adventure Instructor on my return to Ireland two years back.

✦

So, I'm now repeating it all over again and this time it appears there are two people I'm searching for, as Ben's come back into my life, and I might even find my dad. When I was first here my life had gone into free fall (yes, more than usual) following the disappearance of Ben who I had fallen in with along the Way. He was a good sort so don't quite know why he hung around with me. He was doing the walk to raise money in memory of a friend who had died. Or so he said. He never actually explained how he was raising money or how much had been promised. I always thought you got organised before you set off on a sponsored activity but heh, I've never done one or been asked to give. We met in a hostel near Puente la Reina and had walked together, on and off, with Camille; Spanish, on her own and confident, until that fateful night in Burgos when everything changed.

Here I am now having the devil's own job getting my head round a coincidence of mammoth proportions; the person I recently stopped and talked to was Ben's mum, of all people.

What are the odds for that happening? I shared time with her, listened to her story, searched Ben's face on the photo she showed me, kept a secret and denied all knowledge of him. Why on earth did I do that?

Following on from my meeting with her, I realised the next major stop would actually be Burgos and as I walked other thoughts, other people, apart from my errant family, accompanied me. The kindness of Father Dickinson who over time, appears to have given so much support to my family and Peter's mum, who took me in as a youngster when I turned up on their doorstep pretending I was calling for him but in reality, was hoping for a meal and bed. My time recently as an outdoor instructor, teaching water sports, hill walking and climbing, still drinking but managing to hold down the job, thank God for the physical requirements of the training which were now standing me in good stead as I journeyed the Camino.

The Camino? What was I hoping to achieve when I reached Santiago and had to face the consequent need to acknowledge decisions about my future? Then Ben flashed through my mind ... is he alive? Safe? Moved on? Where? I couldn't bring myself to think beyond that. I passed through wooded areas, hamlets – some looking abandoned, others holding on to habitation through their elderly population as they shuffled the streets, sat outside cafes in the sun, chatted with neighbours, all with one intent: to hang on to the days left to them.

Life in rural Ireland, in fact any rural area in any country, would be much the same.

It was mid-morning when I reached Burgos and passed under the Arco de San Juan. Recognisable streets and medieval passageways welcomed me as I followed my instinct. Tourist shops, bars, restaurants drew me in, familiar sights and sounds surrounded me. Two years were stripped away in as many minutes. I reckon it was the cathedral that finally did it for me – in a good way. I felt drawn to its ornate splendour and found myself sitting in the nave being reminded of my one visit, as a teenager, to Dublin Cathedral, which I had always considered to be an extravagance of gold and ornate embellishments. This, however, took my breath away; whichever way I turned there was more riches and splendour. As I fixed my sight ever upwards towards the decorative ceiling domes, a feeling came over me which I can only describe as being of absolute calm reflection. A feeling like no other as my head emptied of negative thoughts. I won't say I heard voices but maybe the next best thing.

✳

It wasn't my father's face or voice that came into my mind (not that I know what he looked or sounded like anyway), it was the face and voice of a friend; my saviour from two years ago. Ben, who was the same age as me but with a sensible head. Ben, who pulled me out of ditches and paid my hostel accommodation on more than one occasion. Ben, whose smile had connected with me from the photo I had earlier held; the smile, the person I had denied knowing. Ben, who I shat on after a furious argument over Camille from Southern Spain. I didn't even fancy her but his sometimes holier than thou attitude got right up my nose on occasions.

I continued sitting as his image hovered in front of me. He – kind, generous and non-judgemental; me – selfish and uncharitable. I know for a fact if I had been Ben and had come upon me, Patrick, ever again, I would be shaking my head in disgust at the behaviour I had previously displayed. We had spasmodically walked together, during which time he bored me rigid with his constant verbal meanderings about Camille. He really fancied her like crazy and what did I do? I spent the night with her, here in Burgos and then flaunted the event to him next morning. I was too hungover to realise at the time what he said when she and I breakfasted with him but I do remember the argument, the exchange of fists and him storming off shouting all manner of threats to me. Turns out he and she had already had a bit of a fling earlier in the walk but at the time she had told him she had no intention of getting involved with anyone.

✳

The voices of many countries brought me back to the here and now. I walked down the central aisle of the cathedral, crossed myself at the altar and left through the imposing doors and down the steps into Santa Maria Square. From there I found a hostel that was already open, had a quick wash and change of socks, which was sorely needed, and made for a bar. I surprised myself by ordering a coffee rather than a beer. I realised I had been completely sober for forty hours – and benefiting from it. The sun beat down on my face as I put my baseball cap on my head. I looked at the vintage posters of the city on the outside wall and realised with a sickening lurch this was the bar where Ben and I had argued. It was as if fate was conspiring to exacerbate my discomfort. I looked around the square as if willing a familiar face, any familiar face, to come into view to rescue me – from me.

Where is he now? Is he alive? And Camille? Where might she be? Now, more importantly, why had I denied all knowledge of him to his mum?

As I sat, I recalled my meeting with Daisy, sitting with a baguette and water bottle, not far from Viana. I had not been in the best of places that morning having lost my wallet the previous night and the subsequent time retracing my steps to find it. I had explained the teitos to her and the discomfort of sleeping in one in an emergency. I drew to mind her face, her reddish hair but was annoyed by not being able to recall Ben's hair colour.

I placed some euros on the table and left the bar. I walked around the city again, scanning faces, searching in doorways and shops, willing a familiar voice to cut through the hustle and bustle of pilgrims and tourists. By late morning I was still drifting. Usually by now I would have made for the nearest bar but instead I was wavering in my intent to move on and find another hostel further along the Way. Although the feeling of calm still nestled deep within me, the city had mentally unsettled me more than I had realised. Unresolved issues, unanswered questions and undisguised guilt swirled in my head, together with the knowledge that Ben's mum deserved to know the truth and that was in my hands.

Then, as if my prayer was being answered, I recognised a familiar face.

'Kathleen?' I hovered at a table close by the cathedral steps where a girl with a bandaged foot sat.

'It is you ... Kathleen? Don't know your name, but we spoke in the woods beyond the border ...'

4

...Three Meet in Burgos

B RYONY WAS NOW nicely settled in Burgos, being the first of the three walkers to arrive in the imposing city. Her earlier feeling of positivity had dissipated following the accident in the wheat field that had left her with one painfully swollen ankle and her pride dented and she was hoping the rest would heal her both physically and mentally. Already she was discovering more about the different aspects of her character as they were being highlighted by circumstances and people she had briefly met. She was acknowledging her oscillating strengths and weaknesses, her annoyance that she had given in to temptation twice through her desire for a few home comforts to help her along her way – but also how she held herself together following her fall. Thoughts surrounding the indecision within her personal life were also never far away.

Daisy continued her steady progress developing a greater strength of determination as she started to engage with other pilgrims. She remained positive in her quest to solve Ben's disappearance and the unexpected meeting with Camille and Mateus – who she still could not believe was part of her being – added vital impetus to succeed.

Patrick? Well, nothing fazed him (seemingly) just as long as there could be a beer at the end of the day, just one ... in the main. His meeting with Daisy had proved a salutary experience needing serious attention.

★

Bryony looked up from her phone to see a red-haired girl smiling down at her.

'May I ...?' and without waiting for an answer the girl drew out a chair and sat down. She looked the epitome of an organized pilgrim with a neat pair of navy shorts and T-shirt and comfortable looking sandals on her feet. A greenish canvas day bag over the shoulder finished the look.

'You're Bryony aren't you? Remember me? Daisy? Roncesvalles.' Daisy looked at Bryony's bandaged foot. 'What have you been up to?'

'Heh. Yes, Daisy, I do remember. This? Oh, stupid me, I fell awkwardly in a wheat field of all things, luckily near a village – Belorado? Did you pass through it? Yes, join me. I could do with a bit of female company, any company actually.'

'Thanks. I'll take that as a compliment,' Daisy replied as she drew out a spare chair.

Bryony smiled. 'Sorry. That sounded a bit rude. No offence meant.'

Daisy ordered herself a wine as the two women reminisced over their brief meeting at Roncesvalles and exchanged stories of solo walking, with its highs and lows.

Bryony rattled on about her journey, only stopping when she realised Daisy had gone quiet following their respective admissions for a bit of luxury to counter the hardships. They discovered they had both overnighted at Santo Domingo and Daisy was indeed able to relay the story of the hens in the cathedral. Bryony then expanded her bad luck story of the wheat field and her desire to reach Burgos. It appeared Burgos for both of them had been the place to break their respective journeys but confidences beyond that lay unspoken.

As they chatted, Bryony's phone rang. She hesitated for a moment.

'Take it if you wish. I can make myself scarce.' Daisy appeared to have an innate understanding of the importance of the call.

'No, no ... I'll ring back later. It's too nice to get serious.'

The comment lay unchallenged and shortly after that Bryony

pleaded the need for an early night and suggested meeting for late coffee the following morning.

✦

It was a quieter Burgos that greeted them. Pilgrims had departed and today's walkers were yet to arrive. Tourists of various nationalities, all sporting cameras large and small, complicated and simple, wandered the cobbled streets as a mix of languages filled the air. Bryony was more relaxed, her ankle looking less swollen and she was happy to agree when Daisy suggested visiting the cathedral.

'You trying to impress me?' she laughed, as she took Daisy's arm for support.

The cathedral was cool, an oasis of calm. Daisy chose to sit awhile within the central nave whilst Bryony, sensing her need to be alone, wandered the magnificent and highly decorated interior until she found herself hobbling slowly. Enough walking for the day.

The intense sun greeted her as she made her way down the steps. She found a bar close by and ordered a cold drink. She lay her phone on the table in front of her, picked it up once or twice, swiping the screen as if willing something to happen. She placed her foot on the chair alongside her and sat back relaxing in the warmth of the morning.

'Kathleen?' a voice rang out. She squinted against the sun as she looked towards the cathedral steps. Patrick – still sporting Marilyn Monroe!

Her mood quickened as she welcomed him to the table. He ordered a beer whilst she explained she was waiting for a friend still visiting the cathedral.

He supped the cool beer and looked at her foot quizzically.

'Don't even ask.'

'Who's your friend then?'

'Kathleen apparently,' Bryony replied with a grin. Patrick looked quizzically at her then laughed.

'You mean Kathleen with the missing son? Real name Daisy – I think that's what she said.'

'What d'you mean … "missing son?".'

Patrick blustered a little.

'I met her a few days ago, we shared a lunch break.'

'You said, her "missing son".'

'Hmm, but maybe I shouldn't tell tales out of school.'

'Forget school tales, what d'you mean?'

'That's what I mean. She said she was looking for her son. Showed me a photo.' Patrick went quiet. 'I couldn't help her.'

'You mean she's doing this to look for her missing son?'

He nodded.

Bryony lifted her sunglasses to study his face.

'Honest to God. Kath... What is your name? I know we don't know each other but what I've said is God's truth. We only spoke for a short while; she didn't elaborate when I said I couldn't help her.'

Bryony told him her name and also confirmed it was Daisy she was waiting for. She elaborated on their new friendship explaining their meeting at Roncesvalles and then again, the previous night.

'She's given no indication of looking for a missing son, admittedly we were both knackered last night and just chatted superficially but ...'

'Sometimes we are but ships that pass in the night, other times ...' Patrick halted and grinned. 'Don't beat yourself up, she only asked me because I said I'd done this Walk two years ago.'

As he spoke, a shadow cast over the table. Daisy stood there, looking down at him, then at Bryony.

'Patrick? What are you doing here?' She laughed at the obvious statement then looked at Bryony who shrugged her shoulders. Patrick stood up.

'Kathleen, I mean, Daisy.' He kissed her on both cheeks.

'Did you get your wallet? I found it after you left.'

Bryony removed her foot from the spare chair and Daisy sat alongside as she addressed Patrick.

'Daisy, you are a star. Yes, thank you so much. I won't bore you with all the grimy details, suffice to say the bar owner and you are my saviours. Is it OK to hang in here with you two for a while?' he asked of them.

'Looks as if you already have?' replied Bryony. Both seemed unaware of Daisy's hesitation.

'Well, you seem two nice ladies, I guess you wouldn't send me packing, would you?'

'The charm of the Irish, eh?' Bryony called the waiter over and ordered three coffees.

Conversation around the journey flowed lightly between the two of them with Daisy sitting quietly alongside until Bryony suddenly switched subjects.

'I'm not one to waste words so, Daisy? Patrick mentioned about your son ...'

Daisy stiffened as silence briefly dampened the atmosphere.

'I'm sorry, Daisy, I hope I didn't speak out of turn, I just mentioned it without thinking.' Patrick spoke to break the silence.

Bryony reached out to touch Daisy's arm.

'If you'd rather not talk, we understand.'

Daisy unzipped her day bag and removed one of her pictures of Ben.

'This is Ben, my Ben. He was here, two years ago, here in Burgos. You know this already Patrick. That was the last time I ... we heard from him.'

A solitary tear fell as Bryony comforted her.

'Do you want to talk more?'

Daisy nodded and proceeded to unburden her story. She stopped when she reached the point where she and Patrick first met, he took over, then suddenly he faltered.

'I wasn't absolutely honest with you, Daisy, when I said it didn't ring a bell. It did.'

'What d'you mean?' Daisy grabbed at his arm as if to shake details from him.

'I did meet Ben long before here in Burgos. We fell in with each other round about Puente la Reina. We walked, parted, met up again, went it alone, met others, you know how people do.'

63

'Then why did you deny him when I showed you this?' Daisy stabbed at the photo. Patrick's face reddened.

'Come on, Patrick, if you know more, tell Daisy,' Bryony suddenly spoke up.

'There were actually three of us.'

The story unfolded. Ben, Patrick and Camille – from Southern Spain, walking alone after her friend became ill. The inevitable happened as on one occasion Patrick had tried to chat her up. She resisted; the drink caused him to become aggressive, Ben stepped in, slightly the worse for wear but still able to knock Patrick to the ground.

Daisy gasped.

'Ben? Hit you?'

'Yeah, but I deserved it. I didn't see them after that. Well not properly. I briefly met up at the hostel in Viana.'

'I stopped at Viana the other night,' interjected Bryony.

'So, it was you? I was there too,' Daisy added. 'I thought I saw you with a crowd.'

'As Patrick said, we walk, we part, we meet again.'

Daisy turned back to Patrick.

'You did see him there?'

'They seemed good together so I didn't hang around, Ben did look a bit ... blathered. He liked his drink.'

Daisy began to explain the conversation she'd had when she visited the hostel. Patrick nodded in agreement.

'... But he was never a drinker at home, he was always at the gym or cycling. I don't understand, are you sure it's the same Ben we're talking about?'

Before Patrick could respond, Daisy took her bag and left the table, Patrick half stood as if to follow.

'Let her be.' Bryony reached across as if to restrain him.

An awkward silence lay between them broken only by Daisy's return.

'Are you sure it was my Ben?'

Patrick nodded.

'Perhaps he wasn't feeling well,' he stuttered, by way of apology.

Daisy accepted his response then elaborated on her meeting with Señora Martinez in Viana.

Patrick continued with his side of the story. 'I'll admit it all then got a bit messy. We did meet again here in Burgos...God knows how it happened but Camille and I ended up spending the night together...I'm so sorry Daisy, this is your Ben I screwed up on... I boasted to him about it next morning. We argued, it started to get physical. Camille stepped in, he left... and I never saw him again. I absolutely promise you that.'

'Then what?'

'Nothing. He'd said he was gonna carry on by himself, needed to keep a promise he'd made, didn't elaborate and as I said, I didn't see him again. Honest to God I didn't.'

Daisy was fighting hard to keep back the tears by now. 'What about anyone else? Was there anyone here you know who might remember him?'

'I don't think so. I never saw him after that. I have no idea where he went. Truth.'

Daisy sat, hunched, playing with the buckle on her day bag. Every so often she shook her head as if processing all the facts offered up by Patrick.

She turned to him. 'You seem bound up in my quest, my journey, so why are you on this pilgrimage? Quest? Whatever? Or are you here for your own soul searching? Come on, be honest.'

He looked surprised at this change of direction.

'Let's get the drinks in first.' He signalled to the waiter.

'Well, if you really want to hear the whole sorry story it's a long one, goes way back, back to my childhood, typical bloody dysfunctional Irish family. I couldn't wait to get away, again and again.'

It was as if a tap had been turned on as Patrick outlined his past, giving a potted version of the whole story, he only stopped to order another beer. He explained his previous pilgrimage (his words), made reference to his dad, then blew his nose hard.

'So somewhere here, Christ knows where, might be my dad.

Do I really want to find him? I don't bloody know. When I actually stop to think, I realise I've not seriously looked for him since I've been here. So maybe the Walk is more important than my dredging up my past. What's the word? Cathar–'

'Cathartic,' Daisy finished. 'I'm sorry, it sounds like a lousy upbringing.'

Patrick nodded. 'At times I felt jealous of Ben when he mentioned his home, his gran and granddad ... and you.'

'He talked about me?'

'Yep, you. His wonderful mother. God, at times I hated you and the relationship you both shared.'

'I'm sorry, Patrick, he could ... can ... be a bit insensitive but now you must see why I'm here. I'm his mum, I must find out what happened. I need answers.'

As Bryony shuffled in her chair, Daisy clamped her hand across her mouth.

'Bryony, I am so sorry. We've completely ignored you.'

Patrick went and sat at the empty chair and gave Bryony a hug.

'So, do you have a story? We've gabbed on, bared our souls, how about you?'

She shrugged and looked at her still swollen foot.

'This you know about, the rest, well, pathetic really. No kids, well ... I mean ... no kids, too much time, husband – possibly an ex-husband, lover – probably an ex-lover –and a tussle between the devil and the angel as I try to prove something to myself. Don't ask, it really is pathetic, compared to you ...' she broke off, reached for a tissue and blew her nose.

Patrick hugged her tightly, Daisy moved closer to take her hand. Tears fell unashamedly, adult tears, followed by laughter, uncontrollable laughter.

'Life throws a load of crap and we seem to have come in for our fair share; perhaps we should set up a stall, do a survey of other pilgrims' problems!' Bryony laughed as if to relieve the unspoken tension still in the air.

'So, we are but ships that pass in the night, as Patrick so eloquently put it.' Bryony looked at her watch. 'Fourteen fifty, no wonder this ship's tummy is rumbling. Anyone for lunch? Then I'm off for a siesta.'

Following a leisurely meal, the three prepared to go their separate ways. Bryony reiterated her desire for a rest, Daisy had made up her mind to find the albergue, ask questions, pray for some positive feedback then visit some of the bars and cafes Patrick had suggested. By leaving the posters around the place someone's memory might be jogged. Patrick was a little evasive in his movements hinting at 'getting back on the road.' He kissed 'his Kathleens' as he called them, suggested they would meet again ... somewhere.

'If all else fails, I'll look out for you in Santiago, I'll be there a while.'

'Such a free spirit,' commented Bryony. 'I wish I was as spontaneous.'

'That's youth for you. Lay their heads where they will. I wonder whether we will see him again? Why d'you think he intends staying on in Santiago?'

'No idea. Now you've got work to do and I need my siesta. I shall leave quite early tomorrow. Probably have a coffee here and then off. Seven-ish. I'm looking forward to the walk across the Meseta – a 'time of quiet reflection' according to one of the books. I'm happy to do it alone or ... you choose.'

Part 2, Burgos to Leon

5

Bryony

I T WAS A relief to be able to lock my bedroom door and become 'solitary me' again, something I had been striving to achieve along the Way. I felt unsettled as I acknowledged to myself that to be alone is different to being lonely and just now, I wavered between the two. I relaxed in my room, briefly returning to the 'outside world' for a coffee, then decided to have an early night. I put on my pj's, sorted my clothes for tomorrow, looked at my phone and lay on the bed. My foot was throbbing, which was not surprising, but the inflammation had lessened and I was confident tomorrow's walk would be achievable.

The room seemed very quiet after the bustle of the evening but it allowed me the space to contemplate the day's events. Too much wine, too many emotions flying, intense conversations with strangers who became friends, albeit for the day. Patrick's words resonated: 'We walk, we part, we meet again.' Will we meet again? I really hoped so. Daisy's plight haunted me. The disappearance of a child, the not knowing whether he was alive or dead, the why? Possibly, the how? Will they ever meet again? As for Patrick, what a charmer of a young man. But beneath this charm I sensed a tortured soul. Would he ever find his father? Did he really want to? What about his mother? Will they meet again?

So many questions, so much sadness. It did put into perspective my situation, which I realised was quite insignificant to theirs. I felt ashamed of the superficiality of my past life and my present situation. I had brought it upon myself, they hadn't.

I was tempted to phone Jack again; to share my walk so far. I wanted to talk about Bryony and Patrick and, more importantly, I wanted to talk about us. We needed to resolve our situation, if indeed it was resolvable. From this distance I realised our marriage should not be dismissed lightly. We had both wronged each other but could we find it in our hearts to forgive and move on? Or do we seriously want to? He had not returned my earlier missed call to him and so I made the petty decision not to try again.

I set my alarm, briefly pondered on whether Daisy would join me in the morning, took a couple of pain killers and turned out the light. A disjointed jumble of thoughts filled my mind. I could sense them travelling through my brain, so many invading images randomly searching for an escape route. I tried to ignore them with thoughts of tomorrow's walk but to no avail. I climbed from my bed, opened the window onto the small, silent piazza and took in deep breaths. I could feel myself relaxing, my head space emptying, returning to calmer normality but despite this, deep sleep evaded me.

By six o'clock, light was streaming through the window and I decided it was a waste of good walking time to lie awake with thoughts for which I had no answers. With my rucksack packed and guidebook in its outer pocket, I set off in the quiet of the early morning. My ankle felt strong but I still supported it with an elastic bandage. The streets were empty save a few pilgrims and workers. I passed a panaderia with the smell of new baked bread wafting. I bought a ham and cheese bocadillo and two rustic tomatoes from a wicker basket outside the shop. They were huge, misshapen, with dried earth attached, straight from the ground – and to think a few weeks ago I wouldn't have given them house room. A bottle of water and packet of biscuits completed my 'messages' as my Scottish grandmother used to call her shopping. Good God, where did that memory come from? My grannie, who I was never close to, has been gone these past ten years or more.

It wasn't until I was walking through the city gates that I remembered my last words to Daisy before we parted. I looked at my watch: six forty-five. I had suggested I would be at the bar at 7.00am, quarter of an hour? To return and wait for her or continue? What if I returned and she had not taken up my offer, that would be a waste of time. The devil and the angel were once more sitting on my shoulders as they had done when climbing up out of St Jean Pied de Port what seemed an age ago, the devil won and I continued walking. The piece of paper I had slipped into Daisy's rucksack gave my number; I was contactable even if I could not get in touch with her.

It was a beautiful morning, hazy sunshine with the promise of light cloud later, the best part of the day and I felt good, physically, mentally, and emotionally. My rucksack was comfortable on my shoulders, my body felt rested and my feet took me onwards. My goal was fairly modest: to reach Hornillos del Camino via a visit to the eleventh-century Hospital del Rey and Monasterio de las Heulgas Reales just outside Burgos. Even though I'm not heavily into the history of places I do feel it important to acknowledge their past and their present and my guidebook made it sound worth a visit. In all honesty, I did marvel at the heavy stone ruins of the hospital which apparently had been originally built to treat pilgrims and now appears to house part of Burgos University.

The monastery was a spiritual retreat for women but not for me I decided; this solitary walking was tough enough! I took photos to show my friends on my return and as I did so, realised I hadn't contacted any of them, I hadn't even missed them or my somewhat hedonistic lifestyle. What did surprise me was an element of guilt kicking in for allowing my own personal situation to impinge on earlier thoughts surrounding the plight of twelfth-century pilgrims. Pilgrims in the true sense of the word, they had single-mindedly taken this Path under circumstances far more arduous than mine and for reasons more profound. Just at that point of introspection my mobile vibrated. I was tempted but ignored it. I would check the caller, probably Jack, when I next stopped; it soothed me to

acknowledge someone was thinking of me whilst I was thinking of others.

'Strength of character, well done girl.' I allowed myself a pat
on the back and gave permission to nibble on a biscuit.
There's always a good reason for having biscuits aboard,
treats are a must on this sort of challenge.

The day's walk suited me; it was fairly flat as earthen tracks
took me alongside endless crop fields. Tranquility was only
interrupted by bird song and distant humming of farm
machinery. Pilgrims came and went with their cheery 'Bon
Caminos' and I realised once again I really was becoming
happier with my own company. Was it only a matter of weeks
ago I was lunching with friends trying to convince them I was
perfectly able to 'go it alone'?

By noon I was thankful for my wide brimmed hat and the
plentiful supply of water. I saw a cluster of stone cottages
ahead and promised myself I would rest a while in their shade.
As I sat munching on my bocadillo and deciding where to stop
for the night, my phone vibrated again, again I ignored it.
Finding where to lay my head was more important ... or was
it? Whoever had phoned was now texting. I still refused to be
drawn as I scrolled through a bed with breakfast website for
the region. I made a call to a Hotel Rural outside Hornillos
and was eternally grateful when the owner, Miguel, spoke
reasonable English and had a room available. He offered to
pick me up if I phoned when I had reached the outskirts of the
village. I felt relaxed as I sat leaning against the wall of a
neglected cottage and decided to take a quick look at my
phone. This was not the devil on my shoulder but a slight
niggle of concern – it was Jack.

'Nothing to worry about, all OK here? What about you? We
seem to keep missing each other, speak tonight.'

With an overwhelming sense of relief, I closed my eyes and
pictured Jack sitting on his favourite lounger in the garden
with a glass of red wine at his side. A wave of emotion unex-
pectedly engulfed me. He was concerned, he had made the
first move, not that this was a competition but it was a fact,

he was missing me. Was I missing him in return? Or as much? I chose not to pursue that line of thought, it could wait.

I took a few gulps of water, brushed the crumbs from my lap and put an apple in an easily accessible rucksack pocket.

My stride that afternoon had a firmness to it, my ankle held up and I felt myself smiling as I marched onwards to my next goal. My aim was to reach the village and phone the Hotel Rural by four o'clock at the latest. Perfectly achievable as the way was easy underfoot.

The horizon was spliced with wind turbines reaching towards fluffy, white clouds hovering overhead, and as I paced myself along the newly asphalted road, the distant landscape took on a surreal quality as the motionless giants were securely planted upon stretches of the green, grassy fields.

At one point I swallowed a fly, choking and spluttering gave way to laughter – my laughter – a sound not heard recently by myself or anyone else. I began reciting, 'I know an old lady who swallowed a fly ...' My laughter filled the air as a lightness of mind overwhelmed me. I strode on, proud of my newly acquired confidence, in myself and my endeavour.

The heat intensified, the repetition of landscape and sound became intoxicating, like an echoing chant. Abandoned hamlets and unexpected hills greeted me. A crop sprinkler showered me with a cool mist and quenched my sun-dried skin, evoking memories of my childhood family holidays.

Along the way, the yellow painted marker arrows on walls, fences and stones and the occasional more formal shell sign of the Camino, comforted and spurred me on.

I was doing OK. In fact, I was doing bloody marvellous.

I reached Hornillos by three o'clock, found the church where I had been advised to wait and rang the number. I allowed the sun to wash over my face and thought of Jack and the call I was to make. One thought led to another – Paul? Was he still in the UK or had he returned to Canada? Why had he not tried to phone? I reminded myself I had told him calls and texts would be ignored but all the same, I had thought he might have tried, then remembered I had deleted his number when in Burgos. So, did this sum up the relationship we had shared? A flutter in my stomach disturbed me as I recalled our times together; the hotel room we used to visit, our desire to search out each other's bodies, our secret fantasies made real. The flutter became one of embarrassment as images of the two of us came to mind. We had shared some good times, but I had deleted him from my life, literally and metaphorically.

My reveries were interrupted by the hooting of a horn.

'Señora ... Bryony?' The driver of a VW Golf parked in the square was calling across to me.

'Ese soy yo ... si.'

Miguel wiped his hands on his shorts and shook my hand by way of introduction.

'Apologies for my dirty shorts, I've been picking the vegetables for dinner tonight.'

He lifted my rucksack and deposited it in the car's boot. I have to say it wasn't his shorts I noticed first but his eyes of cornflower blue which seemed to pierce me with a sharp but friendly gaze. Just fleetingly I worried about what I was doing, getting into a stranger's car but reasoned that as he knew my name and the time we had arranged to meet, then all must be fine.

Within half an hour later, I was sitting in the garden of the delightful Hotel Rural, a short distance away from the village centre, a little off the beaten track with the most marvellous views in all directions. My diary and a glass of red wine within arm's reach and I was in heaven. The distant chime of the church bell with the lazy sound of a tractor in the distance and all was well with the world. If this was walking the Camino my recommendation couldn't come higher.

An idle thought did come to mind though as I realised that if I carried on like this, I would never reach Santiago! This time it was not the devil questioning me, it was the realisation I was at peace within the world and within my world and that is what this walk was partially all about. Did it matter whether I indulged myself en route or whether I took the easier options? Or how long it might take, within reason of course?

'It is a journey I have to make.' I remembered saying this to Jack. My journey towards understanding myself and taking me onwards to the next phase of my life, whatever that meant, however I achieved it – or with whom, if anyone.

The Hotel Rural was quiet. One or two visitors but no apparent pilgrims. Miguel had explained how he and his partner had bought the place some years ago.

'We needed a project. We were visiting my family in Leon one summer and on a day out came across a collection of old barns, in various stages of dilapidation. We were working in London at the time but it was starting to lose its appeal so we took the plunge and returned home to buy the farm buildings. The farmhouse had already been bought without the land but we saw potential in the rest of the estate. If you look carefully through the trees, you can just about see a chimney, that's the farmhouse. The view from the back of this was, as you say, the icing on the cake.'

I was impressed with his choice of idiom and he explained that his partner was English and that they had spoken English most of the time whilst in the UK.

'My partner, Sara, and I worked for the same design company but it was always our dream to seek a more relaxed way of life so we came to Leon, put in an offer and – this is the result.'

He waved his hand expansively across and around.

They had certainly put a lot of effort into the attractively laid out garden with paths winding through rose beds, leading to a rockery where bushy shrubs contrasted with interestingly shaped local stone. Palm trees lined a path leading to a wooden arbour with bougainvillea entwining its way up and over, a variety of different coloured flowers intermingling. The path took me to where all Miguel and Sara's hard work would have begun – a large greenhouse alongside a sturdy shed. Compost bins, bags of rotting grass cuttings, assorted pots were scattered; all evidence of a serious gardener. As I retraced my steps, I passed by well-maintained wooden beds containing an assortment of summer vegetables, whilst sun-kissed baby tomatoes begging to be picked tumbled from plants growing in terracotta tubs. It's not often I am reduced to silence but the beauty of the garden took my breath away. As I turned to look back towards the house, a beautiful red hibiscus with its trumpet shaped flowers caught my eye as it flowered in the shade of an old stone wall. It reminded me of occasions I had tried unsuccessfully to grow one in our garden back home. I sat on one of the benches and allowed the vista to wash over me. Miguel picked a couple of tomatoes.

'May I?' he said.

I nodded as he came and sat alongside offering me one of the fruits. My senses continued to be captivated as the extensive lawn took my eye out across the Meseta, a choice of seating areas in the sun or shade completed the landscape. It was a fusion of the best of an English garden with the openness of the high Spanish plains. A garden to encourage visitors to rest awhile, relax and recharge mentally and physically.

'I feel so at home in this garden, parts of it remind me of my mum and dad, he's a real rose enthusiast.'

'We finished the house just over two years ago – that had been mainly Sara's department; she had originally trained as an interior designer. She was hoping to set up business on her own either in London or here in Leon. I have been working on the garden for the past four or five years. We lived in three rooms to begin with as the house was a wreck. We wanted to immerse ourselves in the Spanish outdoor life, get a feel for the house before attacking it.'

This was the most Miguel had said about himself – and Sara - and I noticed the use of the past tense but he was not forthcoming. She certainly didn't appear to be anywhere around but that didn't necessarily mean anything.

For an hour or so I dozed and let my thoughts wander. The gentle buzzing of busy bees as they flitted from flower to flower and the distant background sounds from the kitchen completed this piece of heaven on earth.

'Dinner in half an hour, don't worry about changing,'

Miguel called from an open French window. I was touched by his easy manner.

I enjoyed a delightful meal of gazpacho followed by chicken paella which showed off his culinary skills, at least I assumed it was his as still no Sara, or any kitchen staff apart from a young girl I heard him talking to. The dining room was empty apart from me and a Spanish couple. Miguel asked if we would care to join him in a brandy; the couple declined and so the two of us spent a pleasant hour talking over a very fine brandy, so I was told. Not being an expert, I took his word for it, and to be honest it could have been 'cheap plonk' as Jack would call a supermarket bargain, and I wouldn't have noticed. I was reticent to offer too much so listened as he extolled his love for their new venture – of Sara there was no sign.

I was conscious of needing to phone Jack but was reluctant to break the easy flow of conversation. I hadn't spent such a relaxing time in the company of a man for many months. At home Jack and I had developed a polite, pleasant attitude towards each other, keeping each other at arm's length, although I had appreciated his support and input as I prepared for this big adventure. As for Paul, well! Conversation had taken a very poor second place to the sexual delights of our secret assignations! I felt myself colouring as I again recalled our time together. What had I been thinking to allow myself to be drawn into such a situation? I excused myself and refreshed my face in the cloakroom before returning to the dining room. Miguel was still seated at my table, with a different bottle of brandy in front of him.

'I believe you call this 'one for the road'. His accent was soft, his few words inviting as he inclined the bottle in my direction. I sensed our connection moving up a gear.

'Thank you, yes.'

Headlights suddenly shone through the dining room window. The young girl popped her head around the door to announce she had finished in the kitchen and her dad had arrived to collect her, at least I assume that was the gist of it as Miguel waved to the driver and answered the young girl. I gave a cursory look at my watch: ten forty-five. One more brandy surely wouldn't take too long? Jack didn't turn in early, there would still be time to phone.

Miguel placed a glass in front of me and poured one for himself.

'Salut.'

We made eye contact as we clinked glasses. We shared a smile and I held his gaze as I gently swirled the brandy before taking a sip.

'Like it?'

I took another sip, as much as to give myself time to settle an unfamiliar fluttering as it was to genuinely appreciate the brandy but I couldn't resist a gentle joke.

'So smooth. With notes of apple and peach.'

'I sense a lack of seriousness within you,' he returned.

I smiled. 'I drink it, I enjoy it. A good night cap.'

I faltered as I realised the potential implication of what I had said but he didn't appear to pick up on it. Instead, a silence filled the physical gap between us.

'Sara died nearly two years ago.' Six words spoken. I looked across at him. 'Sepsis.'

My hand went out and made contact with his. I automatically squeezed it.

'You don't need to say any more if you'd rather not.'

'Something in the soil, she didn't like wearing gardening gloves.'

It couldn't have happened at a less opportune time ... my phone rang, briefly. At first I ignored it, but it persisted.

'Jack, my husband ... I'll phone him ba–'

'No, take it, please. Come down for breakfast in the morning when you are ready.' With that, he stood up and left the room.

'Fuck and bloody shit.' I looked at my phone. 'I'll call back in ten minutes.'

I went upstairs. He'd obviously had too much to drink. I knew it had been the Golf Club AGM and my interest level did not improve as his slurred accusation about my not caring caught me off guard.

I did not initially respond. I looked around the room trying hard to reconcile the beauty of my surroundings and the delightful shared evening, with an angry phone call from my husband of twenty years.

'Where are you? You haven't phoned. I've had a bloody awful meeting at the Golf Club. The house is empty, the gardener didn't turn up, and I can't find my carry-on suitcase.'

Carry on suitcase? I had difficulty processing these insignificant statements, especially the last one.

'I'm fine, all's OK. I've left Burgos and my next proper stop will be Leon but that's not yet. I'm staying in a Casa Rural tonight. Why d'you need your small suitcase?'

I wasn't prepared for his answer, silence ensued. He was contemplating coming out to see me.

'Are you there?'

'E-er yes.'

He was sober enough to pick up on my hesitation but sufficiently drunk to stumble over irrational thoughts.

'What's the matter? Have you got someone there?'

'Don't be daft, I'm about to go to bed.'

'You're late? You usually turn in earlier.'

I rolled my shoulders, five back, five forward. This conversation was not going to resolve itself.

'It's been a long day of walking, Jack. I'm tired, I'll phone you tomorrow. I promise.'

The words were out before I could stop myself. Promises made under pressure were invariably difficult to keep.

I slept badly and awoke early as the sun streamed through the window. Six fifteen and no sound of the house stirring. I was torn between turning over and getting up. Twenty minutes later found me smelling the roses. Sprinklers were busy quenching the lawn and a clear, blue sky overhead heralded another day of ... my muddled thoughts swirled. Had I been asked last night I would have tentatively suggested taking a day to explore or was that an excuse to hang around and hopefully continue where Miguel and I had left off. This morning I knew I had to take myself in hand, I was idling along the Way, I was happy, I was proud of what I was doing but my progress was slow. I was taking each day as it came with no definite long-term goal, apart from finishing of course. Leon, which I had mentally marked as my next major stop, was a long way ahead with a lot of walking.

Train or bus was an option of course.

'Train or bus?'

I jumped and turned to see Miguel approaching, yellow T-shirt and yesterday's shorts, casual and back in relaxed mode.

'You're talking to yourself.'

He had a basket and trowel in his hand.

'Come and pick some vegetables. Early morning is the best time, cool and refreshing.'

'I'm sorry about last night.'

'Why? It was your husband, it was natural to catch up, I'm sure he's eager to hear about your progress. I would if it was Sara.'

I made no comment as he handed me a pair of gardening gloves. In companionable silence we picked beans, potatoes, tomatoes and delicate lettuce leaves grown in a shady part of the vegetable beds away from the strength of the sun. I recognised some of the herbs growing in terracotta pots, I rubbed leaves between my fingers breathing in the aromatic bouquet. Rosemary, thyme, parsley, sage and others named by Miguel but not instantly recognised by me.

'Mine usually come in glass jars,' I laughed.

He offered me breakfast outside but didn't join me. Local honey with warm bread, with a plate of cold meat and assorted cheeses and fresh fruit. It was a perfect start to the day apart from the thought eating away at me. What was I to do? Get back on the road? Have another day off and then take the train part of the way to Leon? The devil was vying with the angel again but this time the devil lay like a stone in the pit of my stomach, whilst the angel hovered around my heart.

I eventually made my way into the dining room where

Miguel was laying the tables whilst humming to himself. Vases of small sprigs of fresh summer flowers adorned each table, it was as if Sara's influence pervaded the room.

'I need to get back on the road.' There, I'd said it.

I avoided his gaze which I sensed was in my direction. I idly straightened a fork then looked across at him. He was smiling.

'Good, I think you've made the right decision.'

I wasn't sure what he meant but decided against questioning the statement. Within the silence a feeling of empowerment took hold. I had made the decision and felt the better for it. I needed time to myself, time to face what lay ahead both on the road and within my personal life. I did not need any more complications. Jack's late-night phone call, coupled with Miguel's sensitivity, had unnerved me. Today was the next 'new beginning'. I really hoped it was to be my last.

I accepted his offer to return me to the church. Within half an hour we were back where I had halted my walk yesterday afternoon. Miguel leaned my rucksack against the church wall and thrust a bag of food and bottle of water into my hand, both of which I had given no thought to.

'Not quite a pilgrim yet.' His light-hearted words broke into an emotional tension I sensed between us. He thrust a business card into my hand and I returned the action with a scrap of paper with my mobile number on.

'Good luck.' We embraced and kissed each other on both cheeks, Spanish style. He straightened a stray lock of my hair; in return I gave him the brightest smile I could muster.

'You're doing the right thing. Can I be honest? Whatever it is, it sounds like you and your husband need to talk. Am I right in thinking a married woman doesn't normally undertake this without good reason? Off you go and phone me if you need anything. I hope you bump into one of your Burgos friends when you get to Leon.' With that he climbed back into his car and with a toot of the horn he was off across the village square towards the road back to the hotel.

I looked at my watch: 10 a.m. rather later than I had hoped. I'd spent a few minutes the previous evening looking at my guidebook and knew I was going to have to push myself if I was to get to my next overnight stop before dusk. Despite acknowledging today's forward plan, I still found myself wasting valuable walking time as yet again I allowed my thoughts to dominate my actions.

'Did I make my dilemma so obvious? Why do I let myself get into situations of the heart? What am I really searching for? Why do I leave myself vulnerable to the charms of men?'

It was the warmth of the church stone wall against my back that drew my attention to my lack of physical action. Now was not the time for introspection, I had to get back on the road, concentrate on my walking. Miguel's words regarding Daisy - and Patrick resonated in my head. I would love to hear from her, to find out how she was faring.

The landscape was still dominated by crop fields and sounds of nature. I set a pace which I hoped would allow for the twenty kilometres to my next stop to be achieved. My ankle was completely healed, I felt physically and mentally strong and as I walked, I appreciated all that lay around me. It was one of the best days I had experienced so far and my steps were positive. There were no steep hills to climb and the track across the Meseta was easy underfoot. A few pilgrims passed me by but in the main it was me doing the overtaking with a cheery, 'Ola.' I was thankful for Miguel's rolls and fruit but did not allow my thoughts of the previous day with him to impinge further.

Castrojeriz lay ahead. I was prepared for a simple bed for the night, indeed welcomed the idea. One night sharing would do no harm, and I needed to be able to hold my head up high on my return home and explain to my friends a few hardships encountered. I found a dormitory bed in a local albergue, ignored the fact it was mainly men, and after a simple meal turned in hoping to get to sleep before the snoring began. I hadn't bargained for such an assortment of night sounds: squeaking beds, bodily sounds, mumbling bodies tossing and turning. Luckily the girl on the upper bunk slept peacefully. I did not phone Jack.

Over the following few days, I walked steadily taking in the varying landscapes. The high Meseta with its earthen tracks gave way to harsh roads; riverside pathways gave way to natural paths which formed an old paved Roman road. I made sure I had provisions and water and kept walking, stopping only to sleep and eat. This section of the Camino was a revelation in that I was at peace with myself, independent and confident of reaching Santiago de Compostela.

It was here that I metaphorically dropped my issues by the wayside. Nothing seemed as important as completing the journey. The discomfort of long-distance walking eroded negativity and I was beginning to acknowledge to myself where my future lay. Jack and I had not spoken since Hornillos and I realised I was not fazed by the silence between us. I knew we were going to have to confront our future life journeys but at the moment it was more important to put one foot in front of another on this Camino pathway. Out of respect for him as my husband and partner, I did eventually send a text promising to phone from Leon. Miguel, I deliberately put to the back of my mind, further complications I really did not need at this present time.

Daisy was the one person my thoughts came back to regularly as I realised I was missing her company. The short time spent in Burgos had given us both the opportunity to unburden our issues and reasons for treading onwards. Aches, sprains and developing blisters were inconsequential and therefore ignored. I sensed a fellow sufferer but had the humility to admit my suffering was nothing compared to hers. I admitted to myself that slipping my phone number into her rucksack had been for myself as much as for her and I hoped we might bump into each other. Anticipation of my impending arrival in Leon, mixed with the firm belief I would hear from her, pushed me onwards and with these thoughts the kilometres passed underfoot.

The pilgrim bridge finally heralded my entry into Leon. I found attic accommodation which suited me just fine, small but newly furnished, three floors up in a recently restored house off the Avenue Lancia. It was yet another landscape to appreciate as I craned my neck through the skylight to allow a view of red tiled rooftops, cramped housing and the spire of the cathedral. Barking dogs and neighbourly voices carried through the twisting streets below, whilst the incessant whine of scooters and hooting of car horns put paid to any hope for a peaceful stay. I had decided I would stop over for one night, possibly two if Daisy or heaven forbid, Patrick, appeared on the scene. There was so much to see and I admit I was a little disappointed not to have heard from her and conjured up various reasons as to why, some positive, others not. To have shared exploring the city would have enriched the experience but it seemed as if it was not meant to be. I unpacked my rucksack, enjoyed a gloriously hot shower and changed into fresh clothes. It was a relief to get out of my walking boots, they were serving me well but were hot and restricting compared to light sandals. I debated whether to rinse through some clothes but decided that could be done on my return to the room. Jack popped into my mind and popped out again. Later would do.

The spire of the cathedral beckoned and I set off through the old city with its cobbled plazas. I experienced a sense of déjà vu as the splendour of the Gothic cathedral opened up my memory of the short time I had spent in Burgos with Daisy and Patrick.

It was still warm and I sat awhile soaking up my surroundings listening to the accents and languages from around the world mingling with the sound of the city traffic. My eyes drooped as I allowed the atmosphere to wash over me. My reverie was interrupted by the vibration of my mobile in my trouser pocket. Another missed call and I hadn't even heard the first one. Jack? Friends from home? Miguel? I didn't recognise the number.

I pressed the green phone symbol on the screen to hear a lot of scrambling and puffing as if the phone was in an awkward place for retrieval.

'Hello?'

Surely not Daisy?

'Hello,' I replied.

'Bryony? It's me, Daisy, Burgos. I'm sorry I missed you. I'm close to Leon, where are you? I found your piece of paper and I wanted to phone before but ... oh Bryony ... I need a sympathetic ear.'

We can all remember a time when the angel was sitting on the wrong shoulder for the right reason, me more than anyone! And I told her so.

'I'm already here. Is there a train or bus or taxi? Anything to get you here quicker? I promise I'll wait, there's loads to do, I shall enjoy relaxing and being a tourist for a while.'

I offered to investigate travel options but she was happy to do this for herself. Her voice gave nothing away but I detected a high-pitched excitement delivered with an element of hesitancy. To say I was curious was an understatement.

I had intended visiting the cathedral but now decided to wait and share the experience with her – just as I had hoped. Was the angel rewarding me? Or was I reading too much into the situation – whatever it may be? To pass the time I returned to my room and washed out my socks and smalls. I then strolled the narrow streets in the late afternoon sun and sat awhile in a bar to savour the atmosphere and watch the world go by. With luck, it hopefully wouldn't be too long before a bus journey would reunite the pair of us.

6

Daisy

URGOS HAD NOT disappointed me. For the first time since setting out on the Camino, I had opened up to strangers who became friends. Ben's name was now 'out there', and with luck was waiting to be shared by others. With this in mind I knew I had to keep looking, showing and asking and I was excited as to what may lay ahead on the next phase of the walk. Surprisingly I slept well, even though my brain was in overdrive.

Bryony's last words resonated as I recalled her invitation to join her – my choice; I chose to walk with her. I set my alarm and slept right through it. A lick and a promise for a wash, a hasty gathering of clothes into my rucksack and I headed for the bar, seven fifteen but no sign of her. I was a little disappointed but more annoyed with myself. Bryony's need to get started was completely understandable.

I had enjoyed the time spent with her yesterday and, even more importantly, had hung onto every word uttered by Patrick about his brief time spent with Ben. His revelations gave positivity to my hopes that somewhere along the Camino I might learn more about Ben's disappearance, and last night's phone call to Mum and Dad strengthened my resolve to assert my questioning of pilgrims along the Way. My feelings were positive and physically I had benefited from the short break.

The previous evening of bar hopping had not produced any results but at the very least I had left posters on tables and spoken to bar managers. With all this in mind I was facing the onward journey with renewed confidence.

With the sun still rising over the city, I decided a coffee was needed to see me on my way and then before finally setting off, wandered the streets absorbing the early morning atmosphere. I ran my hands along the rough stone walls, walked over the cobbles, looked up at the spires and Gothic architecture, all the while seeing Ben tramping these same passageways. The city's past flowed from every stone and I promised myself I would return one day.

I found an albergue, La Casa del Cubo, a sixteenth-century building so named because of the cube shapes at the top of the facade. It was steeped in history but offered a modern invitation for pilgrims seeking an overnight stay. I was not discouraged by a shaking of the head when I showed his photo. Patrick's admission that Ben was not 'in the best of places' conjured up various scenarios with regard to his chequered journey, and any one of them could have been true and accurate – or not. I would not let negative responses dampen my continued quest.

I left a leaflet with the manager who agreed to put it on the noticeboard and headed off, aware that time was passing and my bed for the night undecided.

The weather was perfect for walking, the warmth of the September sunshine coupled with fluffy white clouds enhanced my mood, the phone call home had also done wonders for my spirits. Dad, dear Dad, was all for coming out to join me for a week regardless of the fact he was on the waiting list for a hip replacement, whilst Mum shed tears of relief and said if he came out so would she. Much as I love my parents, Dad's hip was the ideal reason for me to discourage their suggestion.

I had not given up hope of ever seeing Ben again but thanks to Patrick and his knowledge of a different Ben from the one to whom I had kissed goodbye two years ago, his disappearance was beginning to be put into a different perspective. My being here brought me closer to a young adult rather than a boy who had set out with the walking stick carved by his grandfather. I knew that if I did find him it would be as an adult who was learning about life's knocks through his own chosen experiences.

That afternoon brought a horizon spliced with wind turbines, their languid movement mimicking my gradual plodding tread. It was easy underfoot but for some reason this was not aiding my pace. A rubbing sensation on my heel caused me to stop, a soreness was demanding a blister plaster. I also realised that hunger was striking and my food supply lacking. Even though I knew about the importance of having sufficient food and drink before setting off each morning, this was something I was still too casual about, food had not played much of a part in my life of late and this mindset still endured. I made a silent promise to think more about my physical needs; to make sure that each morning I set off, food was in my rucksack.

A cluster of stone cottages came into view where, to my astonishment and relief, one enterprising lady had turned her front room into a tiny shop selling a small selection of food and drink. No cash till in sight, merely a money bag tied around her waist. Our communication consisted of my non-verbal pointing at a cheese roll, which was not as fresh looking as I would have liked and a carton of juice. No need for words as she wrote 2E on a piece of card, I smiled, offered a few 'gracias' plus three euros and continued on my way. I ate as I walked aware no further delays could be allowed until early evening. My feet were aching and I longed for the sight of rooftops. My walk was solitary; pilgrims passed by with a cheery 'Bon Camino' and a wave, which on occasions created a swell of self-pity, but in the main I was content with my own thoughts.

The surroundings were wide open, dry and flat, the changing landscape surprised and delighted me. A field of crops, an abandoned hamlet, a hill that sprang randomly into view.

Bryony came to mind; she can't have been so many kilometres ahead. I pondered on the story she had given and wondered whether there was more to it than she elucidated. Her words reminded me of my own marriage breakdown, the suffering, the lack of self-esteem, the loneliness. Admittedly, I had Ben, which was a blessing, but I still recall his anger at me, his lack of understanding of the situation, how it was my fault, my unkind words that caused his dad to leave. As in so many relationship breakdowns the present parent becomes the butt for the child's bewilderment regardless of how both parents might show loyalty to the other in front of the child. I remembered how, despite our difficulties, Shaun and I always presented a united front where Ben's welfare was concerned.

I hoped I would meet with Bryony again, indeed I felt positive we would. Although we had not exchanged mobile numbers, ironically, I had thought I would ask her when we should have met the morning we left Burgos but it was not to be. My mission so far had been to find out what happened to Ben but I now realised it had been clouding some practical issues not originally considered. I needed to get a balance between the emotional journey and the practical one.

✦

The days merged as I continued walking. My heel blister had finally broken which gave great relief and I chose to ignore the rub on one of my toes.

'Pain nourishes courage'. The saying walked with me, strengthening my resolve to concentrate on the important decisions needing to be addressed. At one point I found Patrick walking with me, not literally but his words 'We meet, we part, we meet again' comforted me.

The Meseta certainly engendered a sense of calm allowing my thoughts to wander. Ben was ever present but the Camino's sparse population also enabled me to confront myself, me – Daisy: Ben's mum, daughter, friend, solo walker. On one occasion I recall stopping by a stream to cool my feet in the gently flowing water. As I sat, I had allowed tears to well and fall. Not tears of sadness, more, tears for myself, for what I was doing, for the pent-up emotions, allowing them to escape. It was a wonderful relief as I remember shouting up into the clear blue sky. The words were not important, it was more an act of self-expression. This had been the most rewarding part of my journey so far, cathartic on one hand but still restrained on the other.

I was now becoming a pilgrim not a solo walker, a pilgrim with a mission as I handed out leaflets to other walkers to the point where few now remained. My next major stop was to be Leon where, amongst other things, I would need to locate a photocopying shop.

One late afternoon, a few days on from Burgos, I decided I needed a decent night's accommodation having stayed in various basic hotels since then. One-star rooms were certainly not my most favourite of stopovers but cost had to play a part in this journey. As much as watching finances it was also important to share in the experience of hostel accommodation with the ever-hopeful desire to plant Ben's name in the minds of fellow walkers or trigger a memory in the mind of the hostel or hotel manager. It did surprise me the number of people who were walking for the second or third time, 'gets under your skin' was one comment offered by an elderly gentleman from Berlin; I promised I would keep an eye out for him on reaching Santiago mentally keeping my fingers crossed behind my back. Although there was much shaking of heads as I produced Ben's photo I remained positive, recalling my conversation with Rosa, the warden back in Burgos.

For many, the Camino is a spiritual journey, for others, a shared experience not necessarily confining itself to the actual spiritual or religious purpose, we all had our reasons. Consequently, I did feel compelled to participate in the shared experience; to be with others from all parts of the world but only on occasions! I embraced mixed dormitories, with their snoring, smelly bodies and lack of hot water but such nights did not make for a following good day's walking. My friends would be proud of me but on one particular night all I craved was quality white sheets and overnight privacy.

I had reached Terradillos de los Templarios where I located a hotel housed in an old monastery. This was to be an overnight of luxury last experienced in the parador in Santo Domingo. I booked myself in, made myself a cup of coffee and luxuriated in a steaming bath with rosemary oil added to the water to ease my aching muscles. As I soaked, I cast my mind back to my stay in Burgos, meeting up with Bryony and Patrick. I wondered where Bryony might be today; was she in front or behind? Was she still walking or had she resolved her emotional issues and given up? What was Patrick up to? Was he seriously searching for his father or drinking his way into oblivion? I hoped I would meet them again.

Feeling refreshed I did a little hand washing and set off in search of the restaurant. It was too early to be open so I sought out the receptionist to ask whether a female English walker had recently booked in. She confirmed one had checked out the previous day.

'An English lady with a man's name.'

'Bryony?' I suggested.

'Si, Bryon-y, I remember. She wanted money changed. We spoke a little.'

My spirits soared; it did not surprise me she had stayed here. She was only a day ahead and I had been under the impression she was not the most enthusiastic of walkers. Perhaps she had given in to a bus ride – or a taxi?

I spent the early evening steeping myself in the history of the hotel with its atmospheric peacefulness then treated myself to a meal in its delightful restaurant. I wandered as far as the bridge over the River Carrión before returning to enjoy one of the best night's sleep I had had in a while.

Early morning found me striding along the Calzada Romana, a Roman road judging by its name but with little evidence to show for it. I tried to convince myself some of the stones and boulders by the roadside might have been of Roman origin and marvelled at their longevity, whilst at the same time knew they probably came from abandoned and ruined stone buildings which are a feature of the Camino. For some reason our roads back home came to mind, pot holes and repairs being a common feature. A lump formed in my throat as it triggered memories of driving a young Ben to school, driving to see Mum and Dad, getting to work, meeting friends, everyday life in fact. To my annoyance my mental fragility had resurfaced. I decided to stop awhile, to restore my equilibrium. I removed my rucksack and took a sweet from an inner pocket. I played with the sweet wrapper folding and refolding before putting it away. As I did so my hand touched my phone which had worked its way to one side of the pocket. I was tempted but refrained. There was nothing to say so why raise their hopes? My mind turned to Shaun; for some inexplicable reason I wanted to hear his voice, wanted him to confirm he too still believed I would find Ben. It pained me he did not stay in touch more frequently, after all Ben was his son too. Negative thoughts swirled as I started to again feel sorry for myself.

One or two pilgrims stopped to ask if all was well with me. One – she introduced herself as 'Sophia, originally from Germany' asked if she could join me and offered a piece of her chorizo bocadillo which I gratefully accepted, having forgotten again to stock up before leaving Terradillos. I warmed to her and felt my negativity subsiding as I sensed a reciprocal need in her. As we enjoyed the warmth of the day, superficial confidences were shared. I showed her Ben's photo, she stared at his face.

'Do you recognise him?' I dared to pose.

There was a long pause.

'No, I can't say I do. I'm so sorry. But ...'

There was another pause, I prompted her to continue.

She explained that a few years ago, for personal and spiritual reasons, she had undertaken the whole Camino and now visited this part regularly staying in Terradillos and walking to explore the region. No details were offered and I felt it inappropriate to delve, if she wanted to say more she would, without my interference. She deflected the conversation away from herself, casually throwing me a lifeline without realising.

Over the past few years, I was the third person she had heard of in this area who was searching for their missing family member. One man had spoken to her in the town; he was searching for his son who had disappeared last year. Two others she had heard about from a local resident during a residents' meeting one evening some months ago. She could offer no more, other than suggesting that perhaps the Camino is an ideal journey in which to reinvent oneself. I wasn't sure what she was getting at – if anything – but it did strike home. Is this what Ben has done? Reinvented himself? But why?

Sophia picked at a blade of grass and began to wind it around a slim finger. The only sound was of a skylark singing sweetly overhead, mixed with this however was the thumping of my heart, not so much a sound more a sensation as it reminded me of its presence.

Sophia looked up at me. 'There is a rumour – no tangible evidence, which has its roots in Leon. Apparently, there is, was, might be ...' she paused as if finding it difficult to continue to put into words what she had already started, 'a cult, although some call it a commune, operating from a hamlet not far from the city I believe.'

'"Cult"?' I repeated. 'Are you suggesting he might be there? I don't understand. not my Ben. Why would he join a cult, it doesn't make sense?'

'I don't know your Ben, so I can't say, I'm just telling you what I've heard. I'm just thinking you could put two and two together and make four – or five, I guess it depends on ...' she trailed off at that point.

'Depends on what?'

'It is said they engage with young people they meet along the Way, young men and women attracted to what they have to offer, whatever that is. Young people who display an interest or maybe a vulnerability.'

'Ben's not vulnerable,' I hotly denied.

Sophia shrugged her shoulders. I didn't interpret it as an unkind action more of an unspoken question. Patrick's comments in Burgos resurfaced, the Ben he talked about was not the Ben we had sent on his way with a hand-carved walking stick lovingly carved by his grandfather.

Tears fell; Sophia stood up.

'I'm not going anywhere, I'll be back shortly.'

Her words cut through my grief as she handed me her unfinished baguette and a packet of tissues.

I became absorbed in my thoughts; they tumbled relentlessly, spilling out, creating an invisible cathartic carpet at my feet. I reached out and picked at them allowing them to slip through my fingers, each telling a story around Ben; his decision to complete the Walk, to raise money in his friend's name. His absent friends, his grief, his solitary journey. The final thought lay untouched. Should we have encouraged him? Was he mentally strong enough to make the journey? Had solo walking exacerbated his grief? Might this have contributed to a vulnerability? Was there more?

'What else d'you know?' My voice was raised, had an urgency which sliced through the peacefulness of our surroundings.

Sophia came and sat by me.

'Seriously, I don't know any more. Whether it's a cult or a mix between a cult and a commune? Some say it's a choice thing, others say brainwashing. Because we don't know, it's rumours only. Some say the place is towards Leon, others say nearer to Santiago. I did hear once it being referred to as 'Casa Bonita'.

I consciously stored the name in my mental filing cabinet of offered snippets.

I shared with her Patrick's meetings with Ben and about the girl – Camille.

'Something happened at that point, I'm sure of it. I don't know if Patrick told me everything. I hardly know him so I can't accuse him of … well, I can't accuse him of anything.'

Sophia looked at her watch. She pulled me to my feet.

'Do you want my opinion?'

I nodded as I hoisted my rucksack onto my back.

She smiled. 'Get on your way, it's four o'clock and I bet you haven't anywhere sorted for tonight.'

I looked at my watch, mild panic set in as I tightened the straps. She stood in front of me and held me gently by the shoulders, it was a caring action from a stranger who had listened.

'Keep going, mentally and physically. I admire you and your determination.'

She paused as she heaved her own rucksack onto her back. I sensed more was to follow.

'Has anyone suggested you might not find him?'

This I was not prepared for.

'I take it no-one has.'

She hugged me. 'Sometimes it takes a stranger to articulate the worst. Here, take this if you wish.'

She handed me a card with her name and mobile number on it.

'I only offer it if I think I might be of some use. We're all on this walk for our own reasons and at the end of the day we're all solo walkers. Don't think you have to contact me. This might be useful too.'

She handed me a bottle of water and a protein bar and with that she strode off, in the opposite direction, back towards Terradillos.

'And don't forget your family back home.'

As her final words drifted on the breeze, I realised that after her introduction she had not spoken about herself, neither had I asked.

I gathered myself together, her words resonated as I felt an emotional shift in gear. How could one person, never met before, understand what was going on in my head? I read the details on the offered card before tucking it into a side pocket. Having those felt like a protected shield around me, even if I didn't have the need to take up her offer.

The map in my guidebook told me it was seventy kilometres to Leon, three good walking days. The sun had lost its intensity and I needed to find a bed for the night, the next three days could be contemplated after a good night's rest. The path was easy underfoot as I walked through an agricultural landscape. My mind was buzzing following my meeting with Sophia; so many questions, so many conflicting emotions, so many conversations vying with each other.

I reached Sahagún hardly aware of my surroundings and found a bed for the night in a hostal. I had recently discovered from my guidebook that this type of accommodation offered a little more than a hostel and a little less than a hotel which suited me and my purse, admirably. The simple room over-looked one of the plazas and, just as important, was the shower, slightly cracked tiling but with plenty of hot water to ease my aching muscles.

I needed to share the latest revelations and Sophia's last words to me resonated, another phone call home was para-mount, after I had eaten. Later I sat outside a bar with a half carafe of white wine. Thankfully it was quiet; I had read that this was more a short-break town as pilgrims headed for Hermanillos.

'Hi, it's me.' I gulped back yet another stream of tears as, in great detail, I poured out my meeting with Sophia. Mum and Dad patiently listened; I could hear Mum gulping back her emotions to match mine. How I just wanted – needed – to be hugged and I sensed Mum realised it.

'We're all behind you, every step of the way. Give yourself a hug from us, I know, it's not the same but it will have to do. Are you smiling now?'

I smiled.

'Yes, I am.'

We agreed I would phone again when I reached Leon unless anything happened before then.

Karen, my best friend, listened just as patiently; as friends from our primary school days there were no secrets we kept from each other.

'I'm with you in spirit kiddo but I'm not offering to come out to Spain.'

I laughed – Kiddo, her pet name for me. That statement was typically her, we were close, but in many ways also so dissim-ilar.

'Have you phoned Shaun?'

'I'm thinking about it. I might wait until ... oh, I don't know, Karen. What d'you think? I mean, he is Ben's dad ...' I tailed off.

She paused. 'Have you anything of consequence to say?'

'Not really. I've told you and Mum and Dad about Sophia but – it may have some relevance or may not.'

'In that case, I think I'd hold on.'

As always, she put life into perspective for me.

'I miss you all.' The words came out spontaneously. My guard was down again as my emotions surfaced. 'Oh, bugger, bugger, bugger! I vowed I wouldn't. Ignore that ... Karen? Are you there? Are you crying?'

Silence.

'Karen?'

'Bloody hell, Dais. You're starting me off.'

We laughed and cried together.

I became aware of cursory glances from others seated nearby. The church bell tolled bringing me back to the dusk of my surroundings.

'It's getting late. I'm going now. Thanks for listening, for being you. Love you forever.'

'And you, Kiddo.'

I sat, gathering my composure. I felt drained but at peace within myself. Meeting Sophia, speaking with Mum and Dad and Karen, I felt surrounded by love and support. I was ready to move on. Ben was somewhere, I was sure. Maybe he'd be in touch when he was good and ready, if not, I would face that at the time.

I paid for my coffee and as I turned to head back to my room the Puente Canto bridge beckoned me through the stillness of the dusk; a solid five-arch Roman structure that had been the crossing point over the River Cea for so many years. I stood at its centre to watch the waters below flow lazily under the arches. So many people with so many stories must have trod this bridge, I was one more who could add my own. I felt the warmth of the stone beneath my hand as I said goodnight to Ben. My bed beckoned but not before I had turned to my diary. Karen had reminded me, made me feel guilty at my laziness. As I dug it out a small card dropped to the floor and as I picked it up Sophia's name became apparent, with her mobile number and 'Just in case' written beneath her name. I was moved by her thoughtfulness and recalled her wise words. Today had been a turning point in my journey; so much now put into perspective and I was buoyed up to continue my search next morning. I allowed a 'maybe' to creep into my thoughts without a huge knot forming in my stomach.

✦

The sun streamed through the window. I looked at my watch: 6.30am. I had slept solidly for seven and a half hour hours and felt rejuvenated physically and mentally. Sophia's conversation came to mind and I was determined to keep an eye out for signs of a commune although I wasn't at all sure what to look for. It would be far too convenient to find a large building situated by the road with 'Commune' written on a board outside! My spirits were high, my mind was buzzing. The day's walking appeared to be reasonable, not too much in the way of hills, and before I set off, I had sought out a shop and stocked up with water and snacks for lunch.

CASA ONITA – a place name, flaking paint on a half hidden and ageing wooden sign with letters faint and a partly missing B. Surely not? The name resonated as my heart skipped a beat. Yesterday, Sophia from Terradillos, her words, her knowledge of the Walk, her kindness. How strange she'd said near to Leon not near to where we had met, I chose not to read anything into that. The sign directed me up a lane off the main track I was following, rough under foot with overhanging branches eager to catch at my sunhat. A barking dog stopped me in my tracks as a collection of ancient stone buildings came into view; a pushchair was by the front door of one of the buildings. Before I had time to knock, a young girl appeared wiping her hands on a long colourful skirt. A black camisole top and bare feet completed a casual hippy-like appearance.

'Hola.'

I returned her greeting and in simple words explained my presence. I chose not to mention Sophia, merely explained my curiosity and hope that it might be a place to buy food (a little justified lie!) and how I had noticed the Casa Bonita sign at the bottom of the lane. I heard myself talking too fast, almost tripping over what I was saying. She appeared to understand but responded in Spanish.

'Un momento.'

I stood and waited. The baby began to whimper in its sleep. I found myself rocking the pushchair gently, gazing at the lightly tanned face.

Eventually the girl returned with a young man who spoke good English. He shook hands, introducing himself as Nicolas and I was offered coffee and cake. We sat in the shade of a tree near to the pushchair and I watched as two friendly sparrows hopped at our feet.

'They know when crumbs are around,' Nicolas said.

I didn't reply, there was no need. A feeling of peace over-whelmed me, from my toes to the top of my head, through my limbs, my bones, my whole being. A sensation never experi-enced. I sensed their understanding of my inner grief and I appreciated the silence.

'If you wish to stay the night, you are very welcome, Camille will make up a bed, we have a spare room.'

The words jolted ... Camille?

'I ... er ... thank you, yes.'

'You seem tired, have you walked far today?'

I nodded.

'You walk alone?'

'Yes ... I ...'

I couldn't. I couldn't say what I wanted to. Ben's photo remained in my rucksack. My heart raced.

'Camille, that's a pretty name,' I finally ventured. She nod-ded as if in agreement and asked of my name.

'And the baby?' I pointed to the slumbering little one.

'Mateus, Mateus George,' Camille replied.

'George?'

'Si, his grandfather.'

I looked across at Nicolas and before I could utter a word he grinned.

'Mateus is not mine, it's not my father's name. Camille stays here with him alone.'

George – my ex-husband Shaun – Ben's father, his middle name. I was at a loss. I tried to breathe calmly, unobtrusively matching my intake to my exhale. I wanted to ask more, but again I couldn't.

No more was forthcoming. Another young lad approached carrying a tray of giant tomatoes, dried earth clinging to them as if freshly picked. The type bought from a local village shop or one of the stalls along the Way, misshapen but delicious. Nicolas spoke to him, then excused himself citing work to be done.

Mateus stirred.

'May I?'

Camille nodded. I picked up her precious bundle scanning his face intently. His bluey green eyes stared up at me. What was he thinking? What was I thinking? He wriggled his limbs with their delicate shade of brown. Fingers, long with tiny, perfect nails. How I loved cutting Ben's. I still have an envelope at home with cuttings from … over twenty years ago.

'"Good pianist's fingers," my dad always said.'

Memories flooded my brain as I tried to contain my composure.

Am I actually holding my own grandson? A ridiculous thought – but I couldn't stop as emotions filled every crevice of my being.

I stroked his tummy wrinkling his purple and black stripy T-shirt.

This time I could not suppress a strangled sound. A pink birth mark to the right of his tummy button, a mark which faded at its outside edge. The same mark Ben has on his tummy. The sound made Mateus jump, which in turn caused Camille to reach across to him.

'Sorry …' I took a deep breath.

'What for?'

'Er … nothing,' I replied. I was shaking as I stood up and handed back her baby.

'Please excuse me, I realise I must get on. Thank you for your overnight offer.'

I ignored Camille's look of confusion. I needed to be alone. I was at a loss to know what to say or do. I needed to go.

I collected my rucksack, thanked her, stroked Mateus's cheek and headed away from the house. By the time I reached the bottom of the track my heart had steadied. I was shaking as I sat down to drink from my water bottle. Birth mark. George. These were too much of a coincidence. Had I been holding my grandson? The baby's face was imprinted on my memory. I wanted to go back up the lane, to ask questions, to hold the baby, to hug his mother, my daughter-in-law of sorts? But I couldn't. Or was it, I dare not? What if I was wrong?

I had to talk to someone. Share this with someone. Help me decide what to do. I took a few deep breaths and another gulp of water. Bryony, or Patrick? I had no details and where might they be anyway? Sophia? A relative stranger with wise words to offer. Karen, my friend at home? Mum? I couldn't bring myself to phone any of them. It was too soon after meeting Sophia to take up her offer. It would be difficult for Karen to really appreciate my situation, and Mum? I really could not raise her hopes. I realised Patrick and Bryony would be ideal listening partners, but where were they? I fantasized over meeting them in Leon, sharing a drink and confidences as we had in Burgos. They would be so happy for me. I then realised I was moving ahead of myself willing my story to have the ending I had dreamt about for so long.

I studied my map, realised it was a little under sixty kilometres to Leon, which meant it would be the same back to Casa Bonita should I choose to return – not too far in the greater scheme of things. My guidebook offered accommodation at Calzada and by late afternoon I was crossing the bridge into town. I have no memories of the path I trod, it might have been stony underfoot, parched fields or woodland. Hunger did not enter my day as I coped with water alone and my thoughts.

The Pilgrim office could offer me an overnight bed in hostel accommodation. Anything would have sufficed such was my state of mind. I didn't bother to unpack, merely had a quick wash, found a bar serving early supper and turned in for an early night on the top bunk allocated to me in the dormitory. My fitful sleep was more to do with recent events rather than the cacophony of snoring and I arose as dawn was breaking, determined to get back on the road.

Even lack of hot water next morning did not completely dampen my emotions and one day's perspiration could mingle quite happily with the next. A slight throbbing of my big toe alerted me to the early stages of another blister and as I was searching my rucksack for a plaster a piece of paper floated out with Bryony's name on it followed by her mobile number. It was as if one of her angels had appeared on my shoulder. How on earth had I had not discovered it before now? I was elated to think she had cared sufficiently about me and my plight. Two pieces of paper, two phone numbers offered along the walk. I recalled a quotation about random acts of human kindness and felt humbled I was not alone.

These two pieces of paper, these two acts of kindness spurred me into action and within minutes I was on the road again. Bryony's phone number was safely tucked into my fleece pocket. It was still quite early and the coolness of the morning powered me along. I found a small supermarket and stocked up for the day. I would phone her after I had covered half a day's walking. I was dying to hear her voice, tell her my news, meet up with her but I was also afraid she might not be anywhere near Leon. Sophia, I would call later, she deserved to hear from me when I had positive information to share with her.

'Bryony it's me, Daisy. I've found your number, thank you, oh thank you. You've no idea…Can you hear me? Where are you? Please, I need a sympathetic ear …'

She was already there! And I was a good two days' walking away.

'Treat yourself, is there a train or a bus? Or taxi. Remember, sometimes the angel is still with you, it may have moved onto the wrong shoulder now but for the right reason.'

✦

I was in the middle of nowhere and Bryony had suggested I ignore the angel and find public transport, and so I did. I stopped the first passing pilgrim, an elderly man who looked as if he could have done with joining me on public transport, who could not understand the what or the where to my question. I was tempted to resort to my phone but resisted. A couple of girls spoke English but could not offer anything apart from asking about a taxi at the next village. Finally, thanks to a Dutch gentleman and elaborate hand signs, I located a taxi which took me to where I could wait for the next passing bus to Leon.

It was a scrubby bus shelter with scratched plastic sides displaying the inevitable graffiti. The bus timetable was barely legible, faded by the sun which hit full on. Weeds grew profusely around it and litter lay scattered. An empty condom packet proclaimed multiple usage and I decided to sit on the ground away from the shelter. The sun was strong and I was thankful for my water bottle and snack picked up at Calzada. It was not a well-used road; a couple of tractors and dilapidated farm vehicles passed by, a few Camino cyclists shouted a greeting and elderly cars driven by elderly men chugged by.

I started to worry as by now it was mid-afternoon and I hadn't a clue where I was. My brain went into overdrive; was this an abandoned bus route? Was I going to have to flag a car down? How far was it to Leon by bus? Where was I going to spend the night? Panic began to set in and I wondered whether to phone Bryony. I didn't, after all what could she do? My options were limited: continue sitting, thumb a lift (something I'd never even done as a teenager) ... what else? Ben came into my mind, had he experienced a situation like this? Had he accepted an offer from an unknown car driver? Irrational thoughts took over. Suddenly, in the distance the outline of a coach, an ALSA bus proclaiming Leon. My sense of relief was overwhelming as I flagged it down, paid my dues and settled next to an elderly lady who was surrounded by packages and bags. We exchanged half smiles and I took deep breaths to even out my racing heart.

Bryony came to mind again. She was right, sometimes we

104

have to ignore the angel and do what's best in the circumstances. I shut my eyes and lulled by the smooth journey fell into a deep sleep.

I awoke as we entered the outskirts of Leon. The cathedral spire came into view through the huge windscreen. A sense of anticipation and excitement caused my heart to race, but in a good way. Leon was busy with tourists and pilgrims mixing with the local people and somewhere here, Bryony was waiting.

I was so looking forward to our meeting, she was just what and who I needed but I still had to find a bed for the night. The bus station was confusing as I tried to find my way out and into the streets. There was only one thing to do ...

'Hi Bryony, I'm here.'

7

Patrick

I LEFT THE two lasses exchanging farewells. They seemed to have hit it off even though both appeared relaxed to continue walking alone the following morning. I had enjoyed their company and more to the point felt relaxed both in body and mind. Amazingly, it was as if a burden had been lifted from my shoulders. My presumed dad briefly came to mind but it was Ben who dominated my thoughts. If I could help Daisy in her search, I would. Whilst not actually feeling guilty about my time spent with him, I did feel partially responsible for his disappearance.

I didn't feel drawn to wander the streets so headed for a nearby park which I remembered from two years ago. I chose an area of green away from others, lay down and was immediately out for the count. Something across my face woke me up. The sun was low in the sky and I squinted through one eye to see a dog's face and a tongue licking my cheek. I sat up, knocking him away with my hand.

'Bugger off you lolloping thing.' I wiped my face with my cuff. I was used to minimal washing on the walk but enough's enough where unknown dog spit is concerned. No-one came to claim him and I had the devil's own job stopping him from following as I returned back to the town.

I found a bar which I remembered from two years ago where some Irish lads and lasses had congregated. I deliberately keep my walking solo but it's always good to socialise come the end of the day, regardless of when that might be. As today hadn't even got off the ground, I decided to count it as a rest day, a day to chill, do whatever I wanted especially if I could hang out with some guys from back home. You need someone to suggest one more drink for the Way. Well, I did! But no likely drinking buddies to be seen. I decided to give it a miss and head off into the familiar narrow streets of the city until I found myself in an unfamiliar square. It was quiet with only a few tourists and one or two weary looking pilgrims seated outside a bar enjoying the evening.

The air was warm and my head was buzzing, an unsettled feeling returned, stuff gnawing at me. I needed to process the extraordinary conversations I'd shared with the two Kathleens, not least of all why I had referred to them in such a random way. OK, so my mum was a Kathleen, admittedly known as Kath but surely I was not going down the subconscious association path? Mother substitute? Bloody hell. I know mine was useless but was I really prepared to override her memory?

Hunger pangs reminded me I had not eaten for hours, I ordered a Margherita pizza and a beer. I looked at my watch: 10.00pm, feck! The hostel doors would soon be locked, I would never make it back in time. Not for the first time I might add, so I was not unduly worried – there was always the park. In the past I might have risked throwing a stone up to a window to waken any light sleeper, but this time was different, I was on my own, I had not palled up with anyone, no-one's attention to grab. Also, not finding any drinking partners I was sober and clear-headed, an unusual occurrence but one I found strangely satisfying. Drink had been my companion for so long here and back home; a way to deaden the heavy load carried for so long.

I asked for a bottle of water. Yep water! The bar owner obliged and even placed a plate of olives and bread in front of me. That's what I like about this country, nibbles to soak up the drink, alcoholic or not. I sat and continued to allow memories from our meeting to surface. So many confidences disclosed, so many emotions flying around. What were the odds of bumping into the pair of them here in Burgos? Three individuals, and I seemed to be the common denominator – in a positive way for a change. I finished off the olives and supped from the bottle. The bar owner seemed oblivious to my solitary drinking and appeared in no hurry to close up.

As I sat, I realised this evening was the first time I had been listened to and taken seriously when in female company. It was also the first time, since Camille, a female had unburdened her soul in my company. OK, in the past Mum had sometimes ranted on at me with her problems to which I usually turned a deaf ear. There had been no excessive drinking, no one-upmanship. No losing one's possessions in a drunken stupor. No embarrassment after the event. Just mature adult company. It felt good. I felt good.

I thanked the bar owner, even left him a tip, and made my way through the silent alleys. I decided to return to the park, it was not far away and I felt relaxed about sleeping under the stars. The hostel doors open early for those who wish to get back out on the road so I could nip in and have a freshen up before setting off again. I soon found myself in the company of a few others who had pitched tents or were rolled up in sleeping bags. Luckily there was no sign of the mutt who had tried to befriend me earlier in the day. I lay down, closed my eyes and fell asleep. It was a restless night, no alcohol to numb the senses, physical or mental. It cooled quite considerably and the ground was hard and lumpy, I may have chosen the shelter of an oak tree but I hadn't realised how hard fallen acorns feel. I also felt a little exposed; regardless of where I sleep, I need the sensation of a cover, however light, over me. Gran always said it was my insecurity and who am I to disagree?

Distant voices invaded my senses, my body felt stiff and my back ached. I squinted to see the sun rising across the other side of the park. 7.00am. I needed to get to the hostel to collect my backpack. Within twenty minutes I had showered, collected my possessions and found myself striding away from the city of Burgos through the arch of San Juan.

It was time to increase my stride and quicken my pace. I had no excuse of a hangover to slow me down, in fact my body felt alive and in need of challenging. From my memory of last time the next decent stop would be Leon, a town large enough to hang out in for a few days or use it as the final stop before Santiago. The distance was about a 170 kilometres and I reckoned on nine or ten days to achieve it. Having no map this time I felt quite happy to follow the formal and informal Camino symbol of   St James's shell which directed us pilgrims – or in my case, a solitary Irish fecker – along the Way.

Bryony and Daisy filled my mind again. They were two plucky women taking on this challenge, not only that, but they were also both pretty cool in their own way. Bryony seemed to have a lot simmering under the surface and I suspected there was more than she had offered us. Daisy, inevitably Daisy took centre stage in my thoughts, grieving for her only son and doing something about it. Mum's care-worn face flashed into my mind with the realisation she must be about the same age as these two. The last time I saw her, the time I stormed out after confronting her with a few home truths, she looked old, so much older. Ravages of a tough life, rough skin, hard eyes, bitter expression. It hurt to acknowledge that she probably wouldn't search if I went missing, it hurt even more to think she doesn't even know where I am and what I'm doing, unless Gran had said anything. Jesus, what a shitty life we've all left behind. Relationships, families, especially mine. The first lines of a poem came to mind. God knows how I knew it but knew it I did.

'Parents, they fuck you up. They may not mean to but they do.'

Larkin, if I remember rightly.

What would be the odds of me bumping into Daisy again before I reached Santiago? I knew I wanted - no, needed to, for so many reasons.

I strode on.

＋

Memories of Ben, then Camille flooded my thoughts. Christ, my past coming back to haunt me. That last Walk, two years ago, done in a fog of alcohol and anger. It's a wonder I finished, much less accepted the certificate to prove it. I'd been a chancer, a bastard with no moral compass inflicting my anger on vulnerable decent kids whose main advantage in life was they had a family that loved them and cared for them. So where is that guy, that friend I took advantage of? Not to mention his girlfriend?

Something made me pause as I strode through yet another seemingly deserted village, evidence of small communities abandoned to the lure of the towns. Dotted around were neglected cottages and outbuildings with weeds surrounding them, with the odd wisp of smoke from a chimney atop a house that looked abandoned. I skirted round unfriendly dogs chained to posts, baring their teeth as if to warn me to stay away. No different to many Irish villages of days gone by. It reminded me of where Gran had once lived as a wee girl.

I took my phone from my rucksack, it didn't disturb me that I had received no texts or calls, I hadn't made any so why should anyone be phoning me? I scrolled down, briefly hesitating over Gran's number and ignoring the last number I had for Mum. When I had tried some time ago it cut out with an aggressive beep sound, my ma reduced to a beeeep. I then came across the two numbers now causing me torment. I was tempted, oh so bloody tempted. I sat on a bench looking out across the landscape to a wood perched on the hillside. Another village lay beyond and I was aiming to reach it before nightfall. I allowed visions of our times together to flash before me, him, her and me. A twosome and a single, a threesome, three singles, every which way we had walked. My finger hovered over his name, it rang and rang, then cut out. I tried hers, waited, was about to close the number.

'Ello.' It was her voice, I recognised instantly the breathy way she finished the word, remembered her voice, her accent. We used to joke if she ever ran out of money, she could top the coffers by offering phone sex!

I took a deep breath, exhaled, steadied my breathing. Her voice resonated, took me back; guilt, passion, anger, laughter, and I'd blown the bloody lot. So busy was I wrapped in the past the phone went dead before I had time to speak. The words I finally did utter erupted without thought and were lost to the Spanish Way.

Mobiles are all fine and dandy but they don't tell you where the caller is hanging out. Where is Camille? Too far out of reach? Still here somewhere? I knew I would have to try again soon, very soon.

I was so busy wrapped in my own thoughts that pangs of hunger didn't surface until mid-afternoon. It was easy underfoot and not too hot so I was making good progress. I realised once again I had no real plan for a stopover apart from the village on the hill up ahead, but being the chancer I was, didn't waste energy worrying. Somewhere would turn up, even if it was under the stars again. Luckily, I had filled my water bottle from the hostel tap but apart from a piece of dry baguette, which I found in one of my rucksack side pockets, food rations were non-existent.

As I stood, an elderly man appeared from one of the cottages I had previously thought to be empty. With trousers held up with cord of some type, a shirt with missing buttons and shoes that had seen better days he and the cottage seemed ideally suited. He reminded me of Mr McConnelly, one of my gran's neighbours back home. He held his hand out and offered something – a brown bag with cold meat and a hunk of dark looking bread inside. God's truth, I actually felt myself welling up as I took the bag from him.

'Thanks, thanks, gracias, gracias,' was all I could muster.

He disappeared as he had arrived, silently, without fuss. I chewed on the bread and ham washing them down with the water and for a brief moment had visions of St James coming to my aid. They always say you are never alone on the Camino so perhaps someone was walking alongside me. Within minutes I was on my way again and with renewed energy, I picked up pace as the hill became closer. I felt good, the outdoors suited me and the weather was ideal for walking. Clouds came and went on a gentle breeze. Thoughts of my future briefly came to the fore and with them my acknowledgement that I was perhaps using the Walk as a way of avoiding past issues, present uncertainties and an unknown future. Such was the lightness of my mood though I pushed these to the back of my mind, sooner or later I was going to have to stop long enough to earn a living and acknowledge my future – but not today. Anyway, more immediately, I still had Ben's disappearance to resolve.

I had not seen another walker for a while, then recognised the path I was taking. I had bypassed a nearby village on my previous journey, no doubt having been told by someone about its lack of bars and hostelries. I noticed the sun was lower in the sky and looked at my watch: 5.00pm, the day was moving on. Soon I would need to stop, to avail myself of what this village on the hill might offer, however limited. With luck, there might be a hostel with a bed for the night, and if all else failed I decided to treat myself to a cheap room. One-star was fine by me. Too much was happening, I needed to stop, process it all; the phone calls, Camille, Ben, my own lack of self-respect, the kindness of the old man, Gran, even thoughts of Mum crept into the mix. A lot of Whys? and Where's?

One-star hostal accommodation it was. I was offered a first-floor room over the street, bathroom along the hallway, scuffed paintwork, lightly painted walls but the single bed seemed clean and comfy enough. After a night under the stars this was fine by me. I looked out the window onto the street, nothing much was happening, a few locals chatting, a few shops selling basic necessities, a baker's and a few neglected, empty premises. All told the same tale as so many other small villages I had passed through. Youngsters moving on and the elderly biding their time until the inevitable; no different from parts of dear old Ireland – or rural life in many other countries.

I turned the contents of my rucksack out onto the floor, smelly socks permeated the air and I realised I had used all my clothes up since my last washing session way before Burgos. When had I last changed my socks? No wonder my feet stank, I bet they were dying for attention. I slipped on my sandals and went in search of the landlady.

'Lavanderia?' I asked, holding out my rank socks and a

113

couple of T-shirts and shorts, hoping she might take pity on a poor, young man.

'Quatro euros.'

'Gracias, gracias.'

I returned to my room and lay on the bed. I looked around; it was small but comfortable. The carpet was worn, the wardrobe sported an assortment of plastic coat hangers, and a chest of drawers with a plastic lacy mat completed the room. The pale-yellow walls were adorned by one picture – the Virgin Mary – watching my every move, just like the one in Gran's front parlour. I was tempted to turn her to the wall but stopped as the image of Gran wagging her finger appeared. I groaned and turned on my side pulling my knees up to my chest.

'Gran, what am I doing? Why am I here? Every time, it's a woman screwing up my life or is it me screwing up theirs? Am I such a bastard?'

As I looked around something struck a chord; my bedroom in one of the many flats Mum and I had shared. The swarthy man invading Mum's life at that time was perhaps, my dad. I closed my eyes and tried to focus; him, Mum, me as an innocent, neglected ten-year-old but the memory was too faint, especially that of the man. Mum appeared, sitting at a table, cider bottle in front of her. I was at the table, words spewing from my mouth, words that described her, words I had overheard – somewhere. A neighbour perhaps? Or one of my schoolteachers? Kids in the street? Local shop?

'Blowsy whore.'

'Poor kid.'

... A slap across the face ... the image was gone.

Emotions were coming to the surface, more feelings I had buried. People from my life long ago and more recently. People I had distrusted, taken advantage of, been hurt by, felt for.

'Bloody hell, Patrick, get a grip.'

I leapt to my feet, grabbed my worn bath bag – a plastic supermarket bag to be precise – and made for the bathroom.

I showered, scrubbed, showered again, enjoying the warm water as it flowed from my head downwards, as if washing away my troubles. I squeezed water from my hair, long over-due for a cut, and padded back to my room, drips turning to little puddles on the landing floor. From the bottom of my rucksack, I pulled a T-shirt, grubby jeans and sandals. I needed a drink.

I sat at an outside table, turning my face to catch the last of the sun's rays. Inside the bar two old guys were watching a silent TV screen, no doubt waiting for the inevitable football match which seems to dominate screen time in local bars.

'Sidra por favor, err … dos.'

Two bottles and a glass and the inevitable plate of juicy olives followed.

'Good man yerself!' I smiled my acknowledgement.

The sun relaxed me, physically and emotionally. Had I really smiled at him? I don't do smiles readily.

As I sat, I began to play name games in my head.

Take names of people you know, match them in various categories. Consider emotions and feeling. Order the names –

In age order

Time known

Good feeling about them

Guilt feelings

Last seen

Emotion towards

I vaguely remembered a counsellor of some type playing this with me. At the time I had no real idea why until later, as a teenager, I recalled my school intervening in my home life. No strong pattern emerged, bar one name: Ben was right up there in my guilt, emotion towards and last seen groups. Camille I was muddled over, I had taken advantage of her kindness and vulnerability thus contributing to a sense of guilt but it does take two. Mum – well. What can I say?

A proffered menu thankfully interrupted my game, I was starving and ordered the largest pizza with a side of garlic bread.

115

The bar was beginning to fill, with locals rather than pilgrims. I was happy to remain anonymous and ignored. A few families strolled and chatted as their children ran and played around the square. The sun was beginning to set below the church tower, an ever-present symbol of village solidarity.

'So, what's to be done?' I realised I was speaking aloud, I looked around but no-one was taking any notice. Names and faces crowded in on me again.

Ben's face dominated. Was he alive? If so, where? Or dead? If so, why no body? This was the first time I had actually contemplated such an option and it hurt – in my head and in my heart. Why did he go off on his own? If indeed he did. How come there was such a personality change after he'd had a couple of bevvies?

Close by a phone rang – and rang.

I realised it was mine.

'Patrick's phone.' The words were out before I had time to consider my normal cheeky style response.

Silence, but I sensed who it was.

'Patrick?' There was no questioning the voice.

'Camille?'

'Si ... yes.'

'How are you?'

'Bien gracias. Fine ... and you?'

I took a long sup of my cider, to compose myself as much as anything else.

'Fine ... thanks.'

'You phoned me earlier?'

'Er, yes, I did.'

'I thought it was you.'

'You put the phone down.'

'Si, yes ... why did you phone?'

Why had I phoned? How long have you got?

'I'm in Spain, on the Camino. What about you?'

'On the Camino? Again? Why?'

'Long story – what about you?'

116

'I'm actually living in a small place off the Camino, towards Leon.'

I looked around almost expecting her to emerge from one of the little houses opposite the bar.

'Bloody hell, Cam.'

There was a silence. I wiped the last of the pizza crust around the plate.

'Don't call me that.'

'Sorry.' It was such an insignificant word but I realised its context weighed heavy. A pet abbreviation from past times.

'You haven't answered me. Why are you doing the Camino again? Why did you phone?'

'Camille, it's a long story, goes way back … and now … not so far back. Can we meet?'

There, I'd said it.

'I've tried to bury the past.'

'Believe you me, so have I, but I've met someone …'

'Oh congratulations.'

'No, not in that way,' I laughed. 'Still footloose and fancy free, that's me.'

The statement broke the tension.

'Where are you?'

'Beyond Burgos … pure coincidence.'

'Have you … have you heard from … Ben?'

At last, the elephant in the room had trumped its existence.

'No, nothing.'

'Why did you phone?'

'You're not gonna believe this, I've met Ben's mum – in Burgos. Look, I really need to see you. She's looking for him. Did you know he'd disappeared? Honest Cam – Camille, she's desperate to hear from anyone who might have met him.'

It went quiet. I filled the gap by tentatively suggesting if she was up for it, we meet in Leon. I really didn't want to retrace my steps back to Burgos, I was here to move on, not back.

An unfamiliar sound came down the phone.

'Ssh …' Camille's voice became gentle.

'What have you got there?' I asked.

'Mateus, my baby, fourteen months old, he's just woken up, I'll have to go. I think maybe we do need to meet.'

Her baby news came out of the blue and briefly rendered me speechless. I mentally counted back the months, suddenly I knew I had to see her.

Her adult voice returned. 'I have a friend in Leon, it would be good to catch up with her, let's make it there. You ring me when you're close by and I can meet you.'

She sounded pretty relaxed about the whole thing; the distance didn't faze her so I didn't suggest any alternative.

'Look, I must go, ring me when you're ready.'

And with that the phone went dead.

I sat, stunned. Faces flashed before me: hers, Ben's, both together. She was close by, with a baba. No mention of the father, mental calculation again. Our conversation and her voice unsettled me. Why had I decided to return to the Camino? Why was it Daisy I chose to sit with so many kilometres back? What were the odds of bumping into her in Burgos? Wounds best left to heal were being opened, but of Ben there was no hint. Unless my meeting with Camille in Leon might reveal otherwise.

I realised I was tapping my foot beneath the table, subconsciously, like a nervous reaction to something. It took me back to my childhood, sitting in Gran's kitchen and her slapping my knee to stop me doing it. I felt the need to phone her, hear her voice, make contact with Ireland but it was too late at night and my phone needed charging.

✦

I was on the road by 9.00am with a rucksack of clean clothes, a cheese baguette and two apples. Señora kissed me on both cheeks and said something I didn't understand. From her smile I guessed it might have been words of wisdom or certainly encouragement.

My 'Gracias' seemed very insignificant.

Although reaching Santiago had always been my intention, I had not set any specific goals for the journey before leaving

Ireland, there seemed no need. Neither had there been any good reason to contemplate staying in Spain, be it Santiago or anywhere else for that matter. No decisions were needed. Those were the thoughts of some weeks ago but as Ben entered my life again another potential goal hovered and it had his name attached to it. However, I also needed a challenge. There is a difference between challenges and goals and I am the sort of guy who needs to test myself, whether coping with that extra bottle or walking that extra kilometre, and with that in mind the forward kilometres beckoned. I needed to make up for lost time as the two days in Burgos and the leisurely overnight stay in the hostal had put me behind in what I realised was becoming a loosely planned schedule. In other words, I needed to crack on, challenge myself to reach Leon – and Camille – within three to four days.

A map in the local bar had shown the Alto de Mostelares lay ahead; a rise of 900 metres, which didn't normally faze me but I was surprised and annoyed that my climb was hampered by aching calves and an awareness of my rucksack rubbing on my shoulders. Although it was earthen tracks beneath my feet the going was hard. My body was complaining, I was paying the physical price for the irregular walking regime of late. Add to that my mental state was wavering; it seemed as if my life was being infused with a mix of emotional feelings – torment, guilt, envy, hope, belief, back to guilt and hope, unfamiliar feelings suppressed over many years. As I climbed, I reasoned that what went up had to come down and if I had succeeded two years ago I would again. I synced my breathing with my pace and acknowledged the journey was more about solving the mystery surrounding Ben' disappearance rather than how much drink I could consume.

I was aiming to reach Fromista and hopefully beyond. No good reason, just a town to aim for. It was an exposed walk through an open agricultural landscape, the flatness gradually soothed my mood and Fromista came and went. I had estimated how many days' walking before phoning Camille and I used the time to assimilate all that was happening. I became aware of more pilgrims ahead and indeed overtaking me, we shared the customary 'Bon Camino' but no more as we each submitted to our various mental or spiritual journeys. I cynically viewed the more well-dressed walkers as opportunists covering the last half of the walk rather than have submitted to the whole ... cheeky buggers out to claim the Compestella on reaching Santiago regardless of how far they had journeyed.

Camille – and the baby – accompanied my thoughts as I walked. She had been evasive on the phone and had not mentioned whether she would be bringing him or her. I couldn't decide whether I wanted to see whatever it was. The word baby in itself was not readily articulated by me, much less my being involved with one, babies never having been part of my life.

'Me – a dad? Never. Maybe? Or Ben? One of us? Neither of us?'

This journey was throwing up situations I had not bargained for. Possibly having to think and act as a grown-up for a start! Me, late twenties, an adult? Never!

I reached Sahagún with ease, booked into a hostel and made for a bar. I kept an eye out for a shop to buy snacks and water before I needed to get on my way the following morning. The town was busy and there was plenty to occupy me, but Leon lay ahead and uppermost in my mind was meeting Camille.

My phone call was brief and her answer was to the point: 11.00am the day after next in a particular bar near the cathedral. An unfamiliar sensation in my stomach alerted me to the anticipation I felt at meeting her. Two years and so much had happened in that time without my knowledge. How should I greet her? Kiss on both cheeks was the norm here so no issue. Should I bring up the baby situation or wait for her? Pass on that one. How should I respond if she had the baby with her? Pass on that one too. What about Ben? I needed to explain about Daisy's quest. So many questions, so many quandaries.

I was one of the first to leave the hostel in the early morning, my head torch luckily still worked as I set off. I enjoyed the cool breeze as dawn rose over the ancient stone bridge which carried the Camino out of town. I paced myself well and after two days of comfortable walking and a little jogging, I entered Leon over the Pilgrim Bridge.

The first thing I needed to do was find an Albergue de Peregrinos. The brass Camino Way markers set in the pavement drew me to the old city and conveniently situated accommodation. The hostel manager allowed me to make a booking for the next two nights and I was shown a single room which surprised and pleased me. I really didn't fancy a dormitory bunk bed. By 10.30am I was in a state of nerves; I'd done a recce and found the bar, wandered the nearby streets, avoided giving in to a beer and found myself searching faces in the unlikely hope Ben might be here. In the end I decided to take a seat in the sun and relax. Camille and I had agreed we would recognise each other but for a joke I told her my table would have an array of empty cider bottles. She didn't sound particularly amused, motherhood had obviously matured her.

8

Meeting in Leon

A TAP ON his shoulder and a familiar larger than life
smile announced her arrival. A colourful scarf was
tied around her head to hold her curly hair in place
but still allowed for escaped wisps to frame her face. He
took in the long floaty skirt and top as he stood and
hugged her. He also took in the fact she was alone and he
couldn't resist a comment.

'No baby Ben? I was dying to say hello.'

Not the most tactful thing to say on first meeting an ex-girl-
friend of a shared friend and Camille's body language briefly
reflected her discomfort.

'I'm sorry Cam … Camille, I'm still capable of putting my
foot in it.'

Patrick pulled out a chair for her and ordered two coffees.
They made superficial chat as they waited, neither seemingly
able to make the first conversational move. The cathedral
clock chimed the hour in the distance.

'Reminds me of my stopover in Burgos,' he commented, and
the tension relaxed as he told her about his Camino journey
and the two Kathleens he had met. In return she talked a little
of her present life. Ben's name finally entered the conversation.

'After you left, we stayed together for a short while but Ben
then decided he wanted to move on and reach Santiago. He
didn't want to be tied down, physically or emotionally, so we
parted. Not on bad terms, more as friends who had reached
the end of a journey, in our case an emotional journey. I guess

you realised that although we hadn't known each other long I had fallen for him and his ups and downs. You out of anyone would have also recognised on the surface he was this regular guy, funny, easy-going kind, but there was another side to him which intensified, you probably remember his moods.'

Patrick nodded but did not interrupt as Camille poured out her memories.

'Beneath the surface he was in turmoil. You were with us weren't you when he told us the reason for his journey ... his friends back home, Mike's death, Sam's illness. His illness. Then him not being well in Viana, I don't need to elaborate, you were there a lot of the time. I also think there might have been more things troubling him, from his past, I don't think things were always good for him when he was at home, I sensed ... oh, what d'you call it ... historia triste ... sadness ... as a child, which he kept buried. I'm not explaining myself very well but do you understand? Then, I don't think ...' Camille hesitated, 'our little fling helped.'

She looked Patrick in the eye, he turned his head away towards the noise and bustle within the plaza.

'I'm sorry.' He turned back to her; she shrugged her shoulders.

'It takes two, and it's in the past.'

Patrick reached out across the table, knocking the bottles as he did so.

'Ever the joker.' She smiled at him as he stood the bottles back into place, briefly resting his hand on hers as he did so.

'We stayed in touch along the way and agreed to meet up in Santiago. He said he was in no hurry to return home, he wouldn't say why, and I was hopeful we might get our differences sorted. By then you had disappeared, never to be seen again.' She allowed herself a grin at that point.

'So, what went wrong?'

'Nothing went wrong unless you mean him disappearing off the face of the earth. His phone became disengaged so I had no way of finding out where he was. By now I was in a bad way as I discovered I was ... pregnant.'

A silence filled the physical gap between them, Patrick ordered two more cafe con leches.

'No, honestly Patrick, the baby isn't yours.' Whispered words, staccato, revealing.

'God, this sounds awful. Which man is the father? How I've let my family down. They waved me off on my pilgrimage, for me to return to them an unmarried expectant mother. Not something to be proud of.'

As she spoke, she fumbled in her cloth shoulder bag.

'They were marvellous and after Mateus's birth I returned back here. I had to do something; I couldn't stay at home. I needed to support myself so I found work at a place called Casa Bonita, not all that far from where we are now. Accommodation in return for domestic stuff and ... here I am. I've tried a few times to track Ben down. I'm sure I told you I knew a couple of friends in Santiago who had bumped into him but that was a while back, then nothing – he seems to have completely disappeared. I live in hope but ...'

She finally produced a photo and passed it to Patrick.

'Soo, the baby ...?'

'Absolutely Ben's.'

Two words and his brief flirtation with adulthood was no more.

He studied the tiny face in front of him. A sleeping babe lying on a chequered blanket under a walnut tree.

Before Patrick could say anything Camille spoke again.

'He has a birthmark on his tummy, so does Ben. Identical.'

'Oh, I don't know what else to say. Congratulations? I don't know how I feel.'

'I'm sure you'll make a lovely dad one day ... don't be sad. We can be friends, no commitments.'

This time it was Camille who reached across the table. Patrick took her extended hand and held it in both of his.

'I guess I'm going to continue the search, almost seems my destiny in life – to be searching. For my place on this bloody planet, for Mum's approval, my dad's whereabouts, Ben ...

Jesus, Camille, life's still throwing me a curved ball and I'm still dropping it.'

'This is all very philosophical of you, but I'm sure whatever or whoever it is you're searching for, one day you will find it or them.'

Patrick squeezed her hand hard, one action that spoke volumes.

They continued their discussion surrounding Ben's disappearance and Patrick elaborated on his meeting with Daisy. Camille shook her head in sympathy.

'Poor, poor lady, I know how she must feel.'

There was a pause. 'Did you say her name was Daisy?'

He nodded.

'A lady called on us a short while ago, took a real interest in Mateus. She was lovely, really sweet. Her name was Daisy. We offered her a bed for the night as she looked exhausted but something happened, one minute she was transfixed by Mateus and the next she was making her apologies and was gone.'

'Bloody hell Cam, sorry, Camille.'

Camille interrupted with a grin, 'Don't worry, I'm growing to sort of quite like it, reminds me of us, the three of us, days of freedom and ...'

'Fun? Can you remember what your Daisy looked like?'

'I'm sure she had red wavy-ish hair, she was wearing a sun-hat, was quite neat and tidy compared to some pilgrims. I can't remember much else, oh, with a dark navy rucksack I think.'

'That sounds like her- Ben's mum -Daisy.' Patrick replied.

They sat in silence as the coincidences unfolded.

'So, what do we do next?' Camille asked.

'What can we do? D'you know where she might have got to?'

Both of them offered various options and finally Camille came up with a practical suggestion – she was going to collect Mateus from the friend looking after him and drive back to Casa Bonita, 'Just in case she shows up again.'

Patrick decided to continue onwards to Santiago and keep a look out for Daisy – and Bryony.

'Can I say something before I go, promise you won't tell me to mind my own business?' Camille said.

Patrick looked quizzically at her.

'Remember, you've got a family too. Stop isolating yourself, pretending all is fine. Your gran deserves some sort of contact. As for your mum ... and your dad ... well, that's up to you.'

Patrick moved to a chair alongside Camille and pulled her to him. 'Is this what having a baby does? Brings out your emotions?'

She allowed him to hold her for a few seconds before drawing back.

'Patrick– God, I don't even know your surname.'

'McNulty.'

'Patrick McNulty, you are a fine fellow. Now go and do what you have to do but stay in touch.'

✦

When the three travellers met in Burgos Patrick had said, 'We meet, we part, we meet again.'

And why not, if the same path is being trod? There are such things as coincidences and fellow walkers do indeed meet up along the way sharing experiences, laughter, difficulties, a drink or two or company over a meal.

Following Daisy's call to Bryony the two girls agreed to meet in front of the cathedral. It was late afternoon when Daisy arrived.

'You and your angel!' she laughed.

'Well, it got you here in record time and looking very spritely if I may say so. Sometimes we have to compromise for our own sanity.'

After hugs and more superficial chat, Bryony wasted no time in questioning their priorities.

'Cathedral or drink?'

'Both eventually, but I need to find a bed for the night first. I suppose you're fixed up in the parador!'

Bryony took Daisy's backpack and headed towards the imposing building.

'I can't afford to stay here,' protested Daisy.

In silence but with a light-hearted smile on her face, Bryony kept walking past the parador until she stopped in front of a three-storey building.

'No parador tonight for me, more of an attic room. I guess there's no harm in asking.'

As luck would have it another attic room was available and it wasn't long before the two friends were back out in the warmth of the early evening sun.

They found a bar in one of the quiet medieval streets off the Plaza de San Domingo and ordered tapas and a bottle of the local wine. Casa Bonita and the Hotel Rural were described at length, their respective times spent with Miguel and Camille and Mateus were shared. Jack was mentioned in passing and the subject of Patrick's whereabouts was inevitably questioned as they each admitted to finding his company in Burgos charismatic.

The subject of his trustworthiness was, however, touched upon as Daisy once again raised her concern over why he had first denied knowing Ben.

Hostel accommodation was laughed over and blisters examined. Inevitably the wine flowed. Each sought advice from the other, each admitted to the earlier fragility of their emotional state, but this was coupled with the realisation they were becoming independent solo walkers capable of self-assertion and confidence to overcome difficulties put before them.

'So, the million-dollar question,' Bryony finally posed the question, 'might the baby be your grandchild?'

Daisy nodded her head, whilst taking Ben's photo from her day bag.

'He has a birthmark on his tummy, same as Ben. His middle name is George, Shaun's middle name – Ben's dad, but I'm not sure how that came about. How many more coincidences do you need?'

'Only you can answer that.' Bryony paused before continuing, 'So what are you going to do?'

'That's why I contacted you. Someone not involved. I can't phone Mum and Dad yet, I don't want to phone Shaun or my friends. I need definitive proof first and someone to share in this. My thoughts are in overdrive, my heart is bursting with anticipation. Camille might have information about Ben, this might be the lead I've been searching for and yes, that baby must be my grandchild, d'you understand? D'you see why I had to share with someone – you?'

Bryony nodded as she emptied the remainder of the wine into their glasses.

'So, what do you want to do? What's in your thoughts?'

'Two words: go back. Go back to Casa Bonita. Confront Camille,' as she spoke Daisy swirled the wine in her wine glass. 'Talking to you has confirmed what was already in my head. Would you come with me?'

Bryony didn't even hesitate.

'No. I don't mean to be rude, this is your search, your journey. The next meeting must be you and Camille, and Mateus of course.'

Daisy nodded as if she knew the answer before she had put the question to Bryony. She suddenly leant back in her chair.

'We've done it again.'

Bryony looked quizzically at her.

'Like Burgos. Patrick and I went on at length and you sat and listened. So wrapped up in our own miseries we didn't even ask you. What's happened with you and Jack? Has your affair with, what's his name, hit the dust? Why d'you look so happy? You look radiant. This walk must be doing you good.'

Bryony smiled. 'Maybe my story this time will have a good ending.'

She spoke a little more about her brief stay at the Casa Rural and Miguel but she played down her feelings.

'I still need to sort out Jack and me, Paul I've not heard from nor given much thought to. He filled a void in my life at the time, he was good fun and sex made me feel young and wanted. Two things I've hardly thought about since I started walking. Putting one foot in front of another has been hard enough work. Sex? Forget it!'

Her frankness and humour lightened the conversation and Daisy admitted to laughing for the first time since she had left home.

'It could be the wine you keep giving me or it could just be me relaxing for the first time in ages but you're a tonic, a breath of fresh air, I'm so glad we met.'

'You deserve some good news, some happiness, and I think – I hope – it's coming your way. I'm not saying you're going to find Ben, I just don't know, and if we're honest, you don't either, do you? But maybe some news will be better than no news. Sorry for being so brutal but you must be having similar thoughts.'

Daisy nodded in agreement, there really was nothing else she could say in reply. She then pushed for a little more detail about Miguel but Bryony refused to be drawn.

'I promise you'll be the first to know when I've got something worth telling.' She upended the wine bottle and placed it with the other one on the table. 'The wine is gone; we've had too much to drink and it's nearly midnight.'

And with that Daisy had to be satisfied.

✦

The following morning found them in a queue of visitors waiting at the west door. As with Burgos the cathedral did not disappoint. Following an unsettled night, Daisy took herself away and sat quietly whilst Bryony, somewhat out of character, availed herself of a headset guide. Light streamed through the magnificent stained-glass windows for which the cathedral is well known; people thronged but only a hushed whisper pervaded.

Bryony wanted to peer inside the Hostal de San Marcos, the parador alluded to by Daisy.

'It's amazing. I can just see myself here,' she whispered. 'Crisp white sheets, lavish guest rooms, fine dining. Wow!'

'Me too. It's like a museum to gracious living,' Daisy

replied, 'but right now my head's thumping and I still need to find a photocopy shop to get some more copies made, then I must get going. I need to find out how close to Casa Bonita a bus might take me. I can't believe what I'm doing, what's happening, but I must go back.'

'Soo, where and when do we meet again? You must let me know how you get on. Do we want to walk part of the way together? Do we want to share entering Santiago or would you prefer to go solo?' Bryony posed the question.

Daisy hesitated. 'I don't know what to suggest. I know I must finish the walk – and finish it with you – but the whole reason for being here is possibly starting to unfold. I've got a lead to Ben, I've found a grandchild, I know for sure, and a sort of daughter-in-law. Until I've seen Camille again, I really don't know what to say or do. I'm churning inside with apprehension and would love it if you were around. I know I'm being selfish but – we'll stay in touch?'

Daisy collected her backpack from the house and Bryony walked with her to the bus station via a photocopy shop. After making enquiries they discovered the bus Daisy had arrived in did a return journey to Sahagun and within the hour they were bidding farewell to each other again as the bus prepared to leave.

'Drink loads of water to get rid of your head and ring me, anytime … I'm routing for you.'

They hugged their farewells and as the bus drew out of the terminus and as if on cue, Bryony's phone rang.

Part 3, Leon to Santiago de Compestela

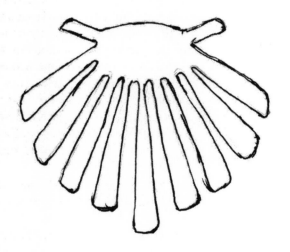

9

Bryony

I SAT ON the edge of the bed stuffing my last bits into the rucksack. My mind was in turmoil, which was the last sensation I was hoping for, following my time with Daisy. Jack's phone call just as I was waving her off had disturbed my equilibrium, and apprehension mixed with guilt over my general lack of response to his various efforts to contact me, filled my thoughts. It was the last thing I was expecting; he was about to book a flight from Stansted Airport to Leon, he wanted to see me, see where I was.

'Just a few days, I don't suppose my legs will stand any more.'

I now had to accommodate him and accept the new temporary walking plan whilst also prepare for this leg of the journey which was going to be a real physical challenge.

Having shared time and more confidences with Daisy, I had felt completely in control of my destiny and was excited at the prospect of the pair of us eventually arriving together in Santiago. The guidebook showed a city bristling with pilgrims and their final destination – the Cathedral de Santiago, and I couldn't wait to be one of them.

Jack's bombshell had now to be brought into the plan as he prepared to fly out to meet me and share a few days walking. He apologised for his angry tirade when I was in Hornillas, and his admission that he missed me came as a surprise or was it that I was hiding this possibility from myself as a way of putting off the decision that I knew I had to make by the end of the walk. Sooner or later, I was going to have to face him whether here in Spain or back home. After all, we were still husband and wife and to all intents and purposes happily married as far as many people were concerned.

'You know walking's not my thing,' he admitted. 'Walking nine holes is about my limit but I miss you. You're out there meeting new friends, challenging yourself and I just want to share in it ... for a few days at least.'

Why had I felt uncomfortable for not completely believing those words?

Briefly, Miguel entered my thoughts. It had only been a few days since he dropped me back at the village, so having had no contact was not surprising and I was relaxed enough about our brief time together to believe he would be there should I decide – or need – to contact him. My mind also wandered over the previous hours I had spent with Daisy. I felt guilty she was suffering with a hangover; I knew she was not a strong drinker and had ignored her less than articulate words as last evening had progressed. I hoped she would be back in control of herself by the time she reached Casa Bonita. I was so happy for her, that at the very least she may well have found an extended family even if Ben's disappearance remained unresolved, which I desperately hoped would not be the case. If I'm honest though, I had also experienced a re-emergence of envy, an infrequent emotion of late but obviously still bubbling beneath the surface. Envy over my friends back home with their children and even grandchildren, and then there was my previous loneliness which I masked in public. Yes, my life has been good, no major twists or turns, no uncomfortable bumps in the road, no really difficult patches so why this response? And why at Daisy's good fortune? She out of anyone deserved happiness in her life. Selfish cow comes to mind!

This walk was turning out to become more eventful than I could have possibly envisaged when I was making final preparations back home. It seemed a lifetime ago, but in reality, was only three weeks. Along the way, I had allowed myself to balance hardship with a touch of luxury, Burgos had been memorable, my injury unexpected but meeting Patrick and

Daisy had more than made up for the physical inconvenience. This emergence of discontent however was unexpected.

With a jolt I returned to the room I was sitting in and Leon itself. I looked at my watch, I needed to get going. Jack had insisted on flying out and I had to accept this. We agreed I would carry on walking and he would phone me on his arrival, at which time we would arrange where to meet up; little did I realise how this arrangement was due for some fine tuning in the near future.

I followed the shell markers on the pavement and soon found myself leaving the city for its suburb sprawl ... an onwards.

I knew this part of the walk was going to be tough with its rise and fall of landscape and places where for long stretches solitude would be my only company. From my guidebook I had noted Astorga, Ponferrada and O' Cebreiro as possible stopping places of either interest or physical need to rest awhile. Having landmarks to aim for also brought closer my eventual meeting up with Daisy and our shared entry into Santiago.

Hostels greeted me as I took on the mantle of a true pilgrim and embraced their basic facilities. The next five days passed in a haze of exhaustion as I climbed the mountains beyond Astorga. The weather cooled the higher I struggled – sometimes scrambling, other times clambering – ever upwards and I was glad of my fleece and long trousers. Villages came and went, some inhabited, some not. Late one afternoon, as weariness threatened the devil to appear on my shoulder, I came across a delightful casa rural. No room at the inn but a chalet in the garden was just fine. I thought of Miguel but refrained from even looking up his number. Truth be told, I was too weary.

Jack phoned me in the late afternoon as I entered Ponferrada. He had arrived. We agreed I would find a decent hotel (obviously) and he would make his way there the following day. I was hoping to feel a tremor of excitement at the thought of his arrival but an emotional flatness felt like a stone lying in my stomach. I was still uncertain in which direction our lives would take, were we going to sacrifice our years together in order to ... in order to what?

✦

I pride myself on recognising a good hotel and I warmed to this one in the heart of the old city. The room opened onto a balcony overlooking the plaza, there was plenty of hot water, the sheets were crisp and fresh looking and the room was of a good size. I noticed a sofa bed under the window which took away the uncertainty of our sleeping arrangements. There was no point worrying about that until we needed to. With great relief I removed my boots and socks and emptied some day clothes from my rucksack. The shower was inviting and an array of toiletries begged to be sampled. I was looking forward to relaxing for an hour or so before heading off to explore.

But then something happened without warning: one minute I was soaking myself, the next minute my foot slipped and that is all I can remember.

I came to with pin pricks of hot water cascading over me. I was lying awkwardly, my head against the shower screen and a searing pain in my right shoulder. My right leg was jammed against the back of the shower cubicle but I was tentatively able to move it. It took a few seconds to take in my surroundings and realise the magnitude of what had happened. Water filled my eyes constantly as it continued to rain down. I couldn't reach the shower control above but did manage to open the door and slither out onto the bathroom floor. The distance from the bathroom to the bed seemed interminable but I managed to crawl across with my good arm taking my weight. Luckily my phone was on the bed and I managed to pull the duvet towards me dragging the phone at the same time.

The hotel staff were superb. A lovely lady on reception answered my distressed call, she came to my aid by gently wrapping me in a fluffy towelling robe and waited with me for the arrival of an ambulance.

I was to be taken to a hospital in Lugo as bruising and a broken collar bone was initially diagnosed by the ambulance crew, but X-rays and tests were still to be carried out. By sign language I managed to get the 'lovely lady', as I called her, to put my toilet bag and the clothes lying on the bed into a bag. However, I couldn't make myself understood as to how far away Lugo was from Ponferrada. I was worried about Jack's arrival but what with the pain and panic about being on my own, I didn't have the energy to do anything about it. I told myself all could be sorted from a hospital bed. I knew I also had Daisy's number but was reluctant to bother her at the moment. I didn't know where she was and it seemed unfair to impose on her my problems. Anyway, what could she do? I didn't need bailing out of my predicament, I was being attended to by the hospital staff and Jack could arrange anything I needed doing (in the first instance anyway!).

The lovely lady reassured me she would pack up my possessions and keep them safe. I explained that my husband would be arriving shortly and would take over my room until such time as it was not needed. She was happy to accept the arrangement.

I was to be kept in overnight as a precaution as the bump to my head concerned them more than the collar bone. I got through to Jack who, having hired a car, was now waiting for directions. I explained the situation, gave him the address and he agreed to phone me from the hotel room.

'The shower's a bit of a mess – bit like Psycho.' He'd arrived at the hotel. I realised I hadn't missed his slightly warped sense of humour.

'How long are they keeping you in for? I'll get directions and be with you soon.'

I convinced him I'd rather wait and he could hopefully come and collect me in the morning. I found myself thinking I was happier to be told he had a car than I was waiting to see him. My finger hovered over Miguel's number. I let my mind wander back to his beautiful garden and the short time we had spent together but refrained from going further. Now was not the time to call him.

Daisy's number appeared. A sleepy voice answered and I

realised just how late it was. I was surprised the nurse had not asked me to stop using the phone. On the other hand, perhaps that was what she had said, in Spanish, when she poked her head round the curtain.

'I just need to hear a friendly voice,' I heard myself saying and then realised how pathetic it sounded as I explained my sorry plight through gathering tears.

'Oh my God, you are in the wars, where are you? I can get to you; you can't be that far away.'

It appeared it wasn't me who was ahead, it was her. She'd had a lift from Camille and Nicolas part of the way and even in my sorry state I was impressed to hear she had climbed to reach O' Cebreiro and was currently overnighting there. Casa Bonita was briefly touched upon; she sounded happy but we agreed to all news on meeting. I dissuaded her from returning back to me by briefly explaining my current situation now that Jack had arrived. I was so surprised she had forged ahead and we promised to phone in a few days. She certainly sounded more organised than me but with maybe a slight hesitation in her voice, and my spirits were lifted when we agreed that meeting at Monte do Gozo was to be a good plan with shared walking those final few kilometres into Santiago. By then my shoulder would be on the mend and maybe Jack and I would have come to some agreement with regards to our future; he may also have returned home. He knew how important it was for me to complete my Journey and that nothing or nobody was to stand in my way.

'My legs work after all.' I wiped my tears as I tried to sound positive.

Daisy's reply was guarded. 'But what about your rucksack? You can't carry that on your back with a broken collar bone. You must be guided by the hospital's advice.'

I hadn't properly considered the problems of walking with an arm in a sling which she agreed was not surprising, she did however come up with the idea of putting the heavier of our possessions into one rucksack for her to carry on our final push.

'Still meet at Gozo. You get there – however– and we'll

make the final kilometres if you're OK to do so. If necessary, use the devil!'

We both laughed at the very idea.

I realised we, or should I say I, hadn't considered how I would reach Monte do Gozo but in my foggy concentration detail seemed irrelevant.

My painkillers were obviously taking effect.

'You need to get Jack sorted. That and your aches and pains are your priority. Goodnight, sleep tight.'

I smiled at her words as the phone went dead.

The following day passed in a whirl of doctors, prescriptions, advice and ... Jack. I had spent the morning worrying about our meeting, what were we going to say to each other? How were we going to be in each other's company? Were we going to come to a decision concerning our future?

He arrived to collect me in the late afternoon looking smart and tidy, unlike a pilgrim, more like a ... golfer on his day off! We were polite and respectful towards each other but conversation was initially stilted. I put this down to the painkillers where I was concerned but couldn't fathom the reason for his unease, we were man and wife for God's sake.

We stopped for a drink in a bar on the way back to Ponferrada.

'You're different,' Jack said.

'I've just spent the night in a strange hospital with a broken collar bone.' I responded.

'No, more than that. You look good, apart from your hair. I know, you've just spent the night in a Spanish hospital with a broken collar bone. But seriously, have you lost weight? You look trimmer.'

Having not stepped on a set of scales since I'd left home or even thought of whether I'd lost weight, his comment came as a bit of a surprise.

'You were always checking your weight, especially after a full-blown meal ... if you can remember what that tastes like.'

'I haven't a clue,' I responded. 'I've certainly not indulged in full-blown meals that's for sure. Wholesome, simple Spanish meals more like it.' I heard myself answering in a rather prissy voice and I think Jack even noticed as a slight wrinkle crossed his face. I tried to make light of my response by putting my good arm around his neck. He looked surprised.

'You have changed. Other priorities by the looks of it.'

I fleetingly wondered whether the statement was a loaded one or whether I was imagining it. I decided to move away from personal comments.

'I admit this walk is taking its toll, physically anyway. Strained ankle outside Burgos and collar bone and bruising in Ponferrada. Luckily no blisters to talk about. Hopefully that's going to be all. Anyway, enough about me, how are you? Have you managed to eat your way through what I left? Have your cooking skills improved?'

He grinned; I had always been enchanted by his smiley grin but somehow this time it had less of an effect. He admitted to often eating out, I didn't enquire with whom and to be honest I wasn't overly interested. He ordered coffee and it was at that point in our meeting that the conversation took a different turn.

'What shape are your emotions in? You don't have to answer if you don't want to.'

His question surprised me, he wasn't usually the one to talk about emotions but the ice was broken. Is this why he wanted to see me? Was there more to his visit than I had planned for?

The journey back to Ponferrada was relaxed. I relived the walk, he talked about his golf but, more importantly, we opened up to each other and by the time we reached the hotel we had been honest and accepting of each other's feelings. Suffice to say we both admitted being more akin to good friends than husband and wife. A great sense of relief was lifted from my shoulders, indeed one that I hadn't realised had lain so heavily.

'Love comes in all shapes and forms and over time it can change. I will always love you, maybe more for what you are and for what you are achieving, than in the physical sense.'

His eloquent take on love surprised me. I guess it was a way of saying, 'I don't really fancy you anymore,' but it didn't upset me. I had earlier mentioned Miguel in a relaxed sort of way and he admitted to 'having his head turned' by a pretty face, which I did think was a strange way of saying he fancied the socks off someone but he was not prepared to elaborate. I was not upset, indeed it made things a bit easier in my own mind where Miguel might be concerned but now was not the time to open up that particular box of thoughts. Enough had been set free already.

The lovely lady had been true to her word and my possessions were now neatly folded and lying in the wardrobe. My toiletries had been tidied away and Jack's suitcase on the bed was the only evidence of an occupied room. It was good to be back in the comfort of the hotel and I felt relieved when he offered to sleep on the sofa bed from the comfort point of view more than anything else. I had difficulty recalling the last time we had made love; indeed my last experience would have been that lustful interlude with … I couldn't even bring myself to think of his name.

We enjoyed two days' sightseeing – and talking.

'Perhaps we should have been more honest when we were together.' I commented.

'I guess we were too occupied keeping up a front where friends were concerned.'

I had to agree.

Being busy kept my mind away from my current predicament. I knew I couldn't continue the walk on my own but felt downhearted at the prospect of missing out on the final stage. I was losing my pilgrim cloak but didn't know how to regain the impetus. I had psyched myself up physically and mentally for this final push through Galicia knowing it was to be challenging but so scenic and now I was to be deprived of the experience. I had also read about the arduous climb to O' Cebreiro and to succeed in that climb and have my pilgrim passport stamped would be such an achievement.

I was mentally not in a good place, I was angry, uncomfortable and frustrated. I was becoming a tourist.

On the third day of my enforced stay in Ponferrada, Jack offered to drive me to Monte do Gozo. We had ruled out sharing some of the walk, for which I think he was secretly relieved, as indeed was I. I was not confident enough and did not want the responsibility of a 'novice pilgrim' alongside me.

My main problem was arriving at Monte do Gozo ahead of Daisy. From my guidebook there didn't seem to be anything particular to do there. Whichever way I turned there seemed to be no answer.

'I could get you to Santiago if that's what you would like.' Each offer sounded more attractive as I sensed the angel and the devil on each shoulder, once again. This time there was no contest. I explained about O' Cebreiro and my frustration over potentially not accomplishing that stage of the journey.

'Then we'll find a way of getting you there before moving on towards Santiago.'

'Then what?' I internalised the question. He must have sensed my unease.

'Or we can just take it slowly. Or … you tell me what's best.'

Those words resonated, 'just take it slowly'. It seemed a metaphor for our current relationship. We had opened up to each other but the final decision was yet to be discussed.

In the end, I accepted his offer to take me to O' Cebreiro and onwards to Santiago. Monte do Gozo was to be ignored, I would get there to meet Daisy eventually, using my own resources which of late had been neglected.

I knew there would be no reason to stay overnight in the O' Cebreiro hamlet and Jack's Santiago offer was, from a practical point of view, a necessity. I had to accept my pilgrim days were temporarily behind me. Fleetingly I recalled passing walkers who had been in a poor physical state but were determined to achieve their goal. I was the first to admit I did not fall into that category. I still carried an angel and a devil and at times their presence conflicted. The journey was easily manageable by car and Jack was more than happy to help.

'You are my wife, after all.'

I let that comment pass and accepted all offers.

My shoulder was still uncomfortable which threw my balance when the going was uneven underfoot but my spirit to accomplish the walk – one way or another – had returned. I would reach Santiago, contact Daisy and sort out the practicalities to enable me to meet her at Monte do Gozo and then walk into the cathedral square with her – as pilgrims.

From the comfort of the car I admired the tenacity of those we passed as they climbed ever higher. On arrival at its summit, O'Cebreiro did not disappoint even though the first thing I noticed was the impending rain clouds building up over the mountain tops.

'Looks like rain!' Jack observed.

'Well, we are in Galicia now, the rainy region,' I responded.

'Glad we're in the car?'

'Do I even need to answer that?'

I smiled to myself as idly I thought we sounded like a married couple.

Jack helped me on with my rain cape and boots as we set off to wander the hamlet. I was glad of his arm as the cobbles threatened to unbalance me.

'It's very Hobbit-y, even the locals remind me of the film.'

'I suppose they must be used to all of us walkers invading their territory but I bet they're glad when winter comes.'

'Yes, but don't forget they rely on tourists – pilgrim or not – for income.'

Somehow Jack managed to bring the magic of the place back to the twenty-first century as I peered into the pallozas, restored stone walled, round buildings with pitched, thatched roofs dating back to Celtic times. I marvelled at how the villagers would have lived in days gone by, sharing their lives with their animals, surrounded by the noise, the smell, the cold and wind in the winter and the heat in the summer. A reminder of how comfortable our lives are today. I was not surprised by Jack's lack of interest, he had never been one for history. We quickly visited the church which was reputed to be the oldest on the French Camino route. Surprisingly, it looked larger from the inside with its sunken floor which we were told gave added protection from the harsh, winter weather. It reinforced again the tough existence but I guess they knew no other way of life. A lady seated at the entrance offered to stamp my Pilgrim Passport which I did not have on me. Jack volunteered to fetch my rucksack from the car and I felt a lump in my throat when I looked through the many empty pages of the Credential and realised how many stamps I had missed out on. Not the be all and end all but they were meaningful in their own right as they reminded me of what I had achieved and, more importantly, become.

I sensed in Jack a waning interest as he intimated our need to get going and I began to realise how our attitude and paths in life were diverging.

We had a quick 'Hobbits meal' (his words) in a simple bar with Jack looking regularly at his watch.

It was nearly nightfall by the time we reached Santiago. The spire of the cathedral could just be seen through the dusk as the rain fell. The windscreen wipers were lulling me and my mood was mixed. I deliberately avoided taking in what was around me, felt no excitement and told myself this was a means to an end, not the end itself.

Jack booked us into two rooms.

'I think we need to stop being tourists, you need to throw off your tourist cape and start preparing yourself for the final stage. Have you phoned your friend Daisy?'

To say I was surprised at his thoughtfulness is an understatement until he spoilt it by saying he had a couple of phone calls to make. Was that the reason for his restlessness? I didn't feel the need to find out more. We shared a simple supper and retired to our separate rooms.

We met for breakfast the following morning. Jack had booked to drop the hire car at the airport and arrange a return flight to Stansted. I idly wondered to whom the other calls had been made. Having spoken to Daisy I was in buoyant mood as she had agreed to contact me when she reached Monte do Gozo within hopefully forty-eight hours. 'By any means,' were her words.

Jack and I parted company with a hug, positive words but no final decision. We agreed I would complete the walk first.

I did feel low following his departure but kept myself busy in a superficial way. I deliberately forced myself not to think about the 'us' situation, biding my time until I heard from Daisy. I bought a day bag and transferred essential items into it to be ready for when she called. I explored around Cathedral Square, noticing the permanent queue of people waiting patiently to gain entry, and made a mental note to suggest to Daisy an early rise if we wanted to attend a midday pilgrim service. Inevitably there were street peddlers, buskers and stalls all encouraging passers-by to part with money; a young girl caught my eye willing me to stop and look. I didn't understand what she was saying but felt compelled to buy a couple of shell souvenirs and some postcards to send home. I was jostled, I lost my way but I did not feel alone. There was a relaxed atmosphere with bars and cafes doing a roaring trade, all the while I kept an eye out for places to eat for when Daisy arrived.

I came across the Pilgrims Reception Office where we would eventually acquire our Compostela certificate and once again noted the queue. I familiarised myself with the process to acquire it and noticed one question which posed the reason for undertaking the walk: religious? Self-reflection? A challenge? I grinned to myself as I noticed there wasn't a box for relationship issues so mentally ticked self-reflection. All the while I surreptitiously scanned faces, hoping two might cross my path. It would be great to see our young friend Patrick one more time and he might even have found out something about Ben, who I'm sure I would recognise were he to be found within this throng. I felt for Daisy so much and shared in her desire to hear word – any word – of her son. I gradually began to enjoy my own company again and drank leisurely cups of coffee, with the odd Spanish Rioja thrown in, with my lunch and dinner.

Being alone allowed for contemplation, on my past, present and future. I was still hesitant to admit Jack was no longer needed to play a part in my life but neither could I make an absolute decision regarding a fresh start. Familiarity in all things is comforting but can be boring. The unknown can be exhilarating but risky, was I prepared to give up my comfortable life to start again? The peace and calm of Miguel's garden, not to mention his quiet positivity, entered my thoughts. I had loved the short time spent in his company and the surrounding countryside had been fuel for my soul. I could see myself immersed in that way of life ... I think. In any case, was Miguel really interested in me or was he just being a perfect gentleman? Did I really experience that frisson of excitement in his company or was I imagining it? This dilemma was not diminishing and time away from home was running out. I was reminded of my inability so many years ago to settle to one relationship; a 'flippity gibbet' I recall my mum once lightly saying about me.

'Come on, grow up, make a decision. You're like a spoilt child, your dad and I have made life too easy for you.' She and I had never shared a close mother/daughter relationship even when I was young, so it surprised me that she even entered my thoughts. Her early death some years ago had been sad but through the years I hadn't missed her as much as I thought I would.

With too much time on my hands I was delving further back into my past than was needed, memories that have no bearing on my current dilemma were surfacing. I didn't need this, I didn't need any more complications.

Instead, I turned my thoughts to Daisy as I reflected on her plight and reason for her journey. I was looking forward to our meeting up, she needed support in her final push for answers as to the whereabouts of Ben and I was not going to leave her adrift in Santiago. A room awaited her, as did I.

10

Daisy returns to Casa Bonita and onwards to Monte do Gozo

THE THUMPING HEAD and the feeling of nausea in my stomach was similar to how I felt when Ben went missing. This time too much alcohol last night was partly to blame but anguish coupled with anticipation added to this mix. Anguish over getting no further towards where he might be, with anticipation of meeting Mateus again – Mateus, born of Ben and Camille.

I recalled how Mum had been my constant; ever present to get me through each day. Her gentle hands soothing away my tears and her calming words offering reassurance of his safe return. Mum and Dad entered my thoughts, I needed to speak to them, hear their words of excitement. Tonight, I would phone, share Mateus and Camille with them, and a photo if Camille was in agreement, a photo of their great-grandson and his mother.

I barely remember the return to Casa Bonita; the coach was not too full and the journey was smooth. The two hours back passed quick enough and before I knew it, I had reached Sahagun. I needed to steady my nerves and drench my dry throat before checking the route back to Casa Bonita so with those requirements in mind I sought out the nearest bar. I was desperate for a cup of tea and more water and whilst waiting for them checked my map. As I studied it two things came into my mind, I wanted to get to Casa Bonita as quickly as possible and I didn't want to walk there. I decided the easiest way was to take a taxi as close to the place as I could and blow the expense.

The bar owner offered to locate a taxi for me and as I waited I mulled over my time in Leon with Bryony which had ended with promises of eternal friendship. I felt slightly embarrassed about how I had awoken fully clothed lying on the bed nursing a bad hangover, with disbelief that I could have drunk so much. This was just not me. I do remember we laughed at the thought of Patrick arriving on the scene to witness two middle years ladies 'knocking back the vino' as Bryony had put it. We had parted with promises to stay in touch and I had assured her I would let her know how my return to Casa Bonita went. We now knew too much about each other to become 'ships that pass in the night'. I recalled how excited we had become when we agreed we should meet before Santiago and that Monte do Gozo was the obvious place and from there we would enter the celebrated city together.

It didn't take long for the taxi to arrive and for me to be set down not far from the track I had previously walked along. The sign at the end of the lane signalled my arrival coupled with the barking of the dog. The empty pushchair was outside the open front door. My heart was racing with a mix of emotions as I knocked.

'Coming.' I recognised the voice.

She was wearing the same colourful skirt and this time her hair was held back from her face by a bandeau of similar material. She looked at me.

'Daisy?'

I nodded. 'How do you know my name?'

'You told us when you were here.'

'Oh, gosh, I'd forgotten.'

I hadn't got off to a good start especially as I then had to request a bathroom visit.

'You left us in a rush, I wondered whether you might return. I hoped you would. You must have heard from Patrick?'

At that point I hadn't a clue as to why she thought I might have heard from Patrick and I certainly wasn't expecting his name to come into the conversation, so answered with a simple 'No' and waited for her to explain.

'Let's sit in the garden, Mateus is sleeping in the shade, shall we join him? I'll get Nicolas to bring out coffee, or would you prefer a cold drink? We have lemonade, fresh this morning from our lemons.'

I could not stop watching Mateus as he snuffled in his sleep. I so wanted to touch his tiny fingers, Ben's fingers, and I sensed Camille watching me. She leaned into the pushchair and lifted his T-shirt.

'Is this what you saw when you were here the other day?'

I nodded. 'I didn't know what to do when I saw the birthmark. Identical to the one my son Ben has. I'm sorry I left in such a rush, it was rude of me, but I panicked. I didn't know what to do or say.'

'I'm glad you returned.'

She took my hand and lay it gently on Mateus's tummy. I allowed the tears to flow, Camille allowed her tears to flow. We were united by this little babe.

Nicolas appeared with a tray, he placed three glasses of lemonade on the garden table.

'May I join you?'

Camille turned to me. 'Nicolas knows all about me and Ben – and Patrick – in fact he knows and understands as much about me as I do myself.'

She explained to me how Patrick had phoned her out of the blue and how they had met recently in Leon, she went on to tell me all they had talked about. It seemed unbelievable that they could not have been far from where Daisy and I had been sharing a table.

'Did Ben stay here at all?'

'No, I only came here a few months ago, I met Nicolas one evening after Ben had left me. We chatted, he gave me a card with his phone number and I took up his offer when I returned to this area with Mateus.'

I looked quizzically at Nicolas.

'I think Camille makes the whole thing sound a bit ... er, how you say ... suspect?'

I smiled at his choice of words.

'I met a lady recently who lives near Terradillos and in a roundabout sort of way directed me here. She was amazing, so interesting, so easy to talk to, so understanding. She mentioned this place, told me that local rumours abounded about it. Was it a cult or a commune? Then, by chance, I found your sign at the end of the lane, almost as if it was meant to be. Especially as the sign is so obscured by the overgrown hedging.'

Nicolas smiled at that comment and explained how he had bought Casa Bonita with a family legacy and was renovating it with the possibility of turning it in to a casa rural. A few pilgrims with time on their hands heard about it through word of mouth and sometimes stayed to help, otherwise he was happy to work alone. He'd heard a few rumours about what Bonita might be but ignored them, indeed found it amusing to be labelled as a cult. He deliberately didn't worry about the sign being obscured, felt that if people were drawn to the name they would investigate.

Camille explained she helped him out and was happy to stay for as long as he could put up with her and Mateus. They both laughed at this and I idly wondered whether there might be more to their relationship than either was admitting to.

'Did you meet Ben?' I asked Nicolas.

He hadn't but felt he knew him from Camille talking about their time together, with and without Patrick.

'I really don't understand him going off like that, leaving you.' I looked at Camille who nodded as if in agreement.

'I appreciate he didn't know about Mateus, but ... I know my son, at least I thought I did and he's never been the sort to let people down, that's why he decided to do the walk alone so as not to let down his friend Sam after he had to pull out. Did he tell you the reason for them doing the walk originally – in memory of their friend Mike who had died from a brain tumour? That's why I'm here now, searching for Ben. We –

152

that's my parents and my ex-husband Shaun, Ben's dad – had drawn a blank over the past months and it got to the point where I couldn't sit at home doing nothing. I don't know what I expected to find, if anything, but doing something is better than nothing at all and at the very least I might find ...'

My stomach churned as I realised for the first time, I was sowing a seed of doubt into my search for him. I bent to stroke Mateus's head, my own flesh and blood, Mum and Dad's great-grandson.

Camille encouraged me to continue and I explained about Ben's father originally coming here to work alongside the Spanish police. How a body wearing Ben's watch had been found which had sent us into the depths of despair. I explained that Shaun returned to identify the body to find it wasn't Ben, rock bottom was reached at that point. We were then informed by the Spanish police that the man who had been wearing Ben's watch was a local homeless person. How it came into his possession we never discovered and the case was never solved, at least not to our satisfaction. I recalled how my parents and Shaun and his new wife supported me when I was at my lowest. The Spanish police could offer no more but the file had been left open. As I talked, I realised I had not contacted the police since being here but Nicolas suggested I didn't worry as they would have surely contacted Shaun had there been anything new. I also talked about Bryony and Patrick.

At this point Camille interrupted.

'I've told you I was with Patrick the other day, that he phoned out of the blue a short while ago, didn't know I lived so near to the city, that I hadn't heard from him since everything went so badly wrong. I was amazed to get his call and agreed to meet. I had already spoken to him by phone, had already told him about Mateus ...' she paused, 'I'm sorry, I seem to be repeating myself. I'm going to be honest with you – he could have been the father. I'm not proud of how I behaved and there's nothing more to tell. It happened and we parted. When Mateus was born the birthmark told all – and his gorgeous long fingers. You picked up on those didn't you?'

Such honesty from someone I barely knew, I wasn't sure

how to react but before I could answer she continued, 'He explained about you being here on the Camino, how you were searching for Ben. I put two and two together from your first appearance and ... well, here you are again.'

She reached across and held my hand and I thought how under different circumstances this young woman might have been my daughter-in-law.

'Nicolas and I have talked endlessly about what might have caused Ben to disappear. We've come up with all sorts of reasons from the possible to the improbable. Each time, for lack of a better explanation we came back to ... Nicolas, you can explain to Daisy better than I can.'

By the time Nicolas had finished I had learnt about an illness called Dissociative Amnesia, its triggers, symptoms, treatment and potential periods of lapsed memory. I had difficulty processing everything Nicolas suggested but through lack of any other options at the moment, cautiously agreed this could be an answer. I was not entirely convinced as we had no evidence of mental health in our family, on either side but, as Camille put it, Ben had experienced mental trauma with the death and illness of his two best friends even if we had not recognised it at the time.

'People hide their true feelings, especially from those closest to them,' she added.

It was at this point I felt angry with myself for not recognising how he had potentially been feeling nor had I been there when he needed someone. I am his mum; I should have sensed he needed help.

This mental condition was the best lead we had so far, albeit with no evidence, and regardless of how I felt, I had to believe in it for now for lack of any other alternative. I couldn't wait to explain to Mum and Dad and Shaun.

Camille confirmed what I had been told by the hostel manager in Viana, that they had been there and Ben had suffered with a cold virus and was acting strangely. This information triggered my memory.

'He'd been ill before he left. Sam became poorly with a

virus, never fully explained so had to bow out. Ben then became poorly, a bit like Sam's virus but not so bad and he insisted on seeing the walk through, he so wanted to keep his promise to the local hospice where Mike was cared for in his last days.'

A soft whimper alerted us to Mateus, Camille passed him to me.

'I need to get his lunch, perhaps you would like to feed him.'

Nicolas also excused himself and we were left alone. His blue eyes, his button nose, his soft brown colouring, his beautifully formed fingers and of course, the identifying mark on his tummy. I was overwhelmed with emotion, the years fell away as I looked down upon my grandson, a tiny Ben.

Later that evening Camille and I sat talking. The setting was perfect for sharing confidences accompanied by tapas and wine and I promised not to disappear again.

'Mateus needs su abeula, both nanas. His Spanish nana is coming here next week. Why don't you stay and meet her?'

I was tempted but the need to get back on the Camino was overwhelming, especially after Camille then told me about two friends in Santiago who had met Ben when they were all together. She hadn't spoken to them recently but potentially it was another lead. I also hoped I might meet up with Patrick again, be able to tell him that I knew the whole story now. He was another strong link to Ben and as the jigsaw of events began to fall into place his presence comforted me. Camille offered his phone number which I gratefully accepted on the proviso she let him know I had it.

It was dark when we finally went indoors. I decided Mum and Dad wouldn't mind a late-night phone call; I couldn't wait to tell all my news, to share Mateus and Camille with them and the latest I had on Ben. I tried to imagine their excitement when I mentioned the words 'great-grandma' and 'great-grandpa'. What a difference one day can make.

What I wasn't prepared for was their cautious response in reply to my bubbling happiness.

'Are you sure Mateus is Ben's?'

155

'We should ask for a DNA test.'

'Don't get your hopes up too much,' ... and so on.

Despite their caution I remained positive that Ben might still be 'out there' as Camille had said at one point. I was happy for them to contact Shaun and also Sam who had retained contact with them whilst I was here. Apparently, he was all for coming out and joining me but I asked them to put him off for now. It did warm my heart though that first Dad and now Sam were offering their support.

I also sent a text to Bryony promising to phone her when I was back on the road. I should have realised a text would be insufficient as within minutes my phone rang. I gave her a potted version of the past hours; she accompanied my words with squeals of delight. I finally came off the phone not quite sure who was the more excited and we had agreed again that Monte do Gozo was to be our eventual meeting place. We knew this to be popular for many pilgrims and coach parties of 'non walkers' wishing to reach Santiago as a day trip, but I had read about a pilgrim statue which seemed an ideal land-mark.

'I'll be the one with a sling,' Bryony joked. 'At least I'll have something obvious.'

Although dog tired, I still needed to write up my neglected diary. So much had emerged in such a small space of time, everything linking to Casa Bonita and its precious inhabitants and potentially further afield.

I finally switched out the light but sleep evaded me. So much had occurred in such a short space of time and my brain was buzzing. Since Burgos, events had followed one after another each adding to the jigsaw that was my journey. Different places, different people, different weather, all adding to the final picture – whatever that may eventually look like. Sophia's face came into the frame, if it hadn't been for meeting her near Terradillos I wouldn't be here tonight. I smiled at the thought of Casa Bonita being thought of by others as a com-mune or a cult; I couldn't wait to scoff rumours. I mentally added Sophia to my list of people with whom to make even-tual contact.

✦

The next morning brought a surprise that completely over-whelmed me. Camille and Nicolas, with Mateus of course, would drive me to beyond Leon.

'Why repeat the journey,' was her reasoning, 'with shared driving we can get you to Astorga in time for you to find a bed for the night. We've also got friends we can always stay over with.'

To have more time with Mateus could not be refused and I gratefully accepted their offer. The journey passed quickly with Mateus sleeping much of the time but at least I could sit and watch his every twitch and murmur. It was good to learn a little more about Camille and indeed Casa Bonita. Nothing offered led me to think she and Nicolas were a couple; they worked well as a team with Casa Bonita at the heart of their involvement but that was where their relationship appeared to end. I idly wondered whether she still carried feelings for Ben but satisfied myself with the fact she and Mateus were now part of my life. We stopped for lunch and Nicolas phoned ahead to his friends; in the end it was to be me not them who was to stay overnight with the couple.

'You'll need a good night's rest before the hard slog begins,' Nicolas joked, reminding me that the next stage was heading towards the mountains and the highest point of the walk. I admitted to feeling a little emotional as I recalled my time spent with Patrick and Bryony in Burgos. How, when sharing our personal challenges and reasons for being here, Bryony and I had given ourselves a pat on the back at our success so far. How we had spent a little time looking at my guidebook mulling over the stages still to be covered, realising the jour-ney was to become more arduous as the kilometres were covered. Patrick mentioned O' Cebreiro which within the guidebook packed no punches; a steep climb but worth it in the end.

'A challenge for you ladies,' I remembered his words uttered with a grin.

Camille rolled her eyes.

'The Patrick we all know and love ... well in my case, knew

and ...' she didn't finish the throwaway line and the moment passed.

I told them of Patrick's scathing comments as he referred to our efforts so far.

'I'll keep an eye out and give you Kathleens a push up if you need it.'

'He was such an ejit,' Camille paused. 'He used to call Ben that sometimes when they'd both been drinking.'

I smiled to hear such an Irish word come from the mouth of a young Spanish girl.

There was no point sifting over old details again but I still found it difficult to reconcile a comment such as that with the Ben who set off from home two years earlier with his grandfather's carved walking stick, full of hope and determination.

Camille squeezed my arm gently.

'You'll get there, I know you will. Don't let Ben dominate your every minute though. I'm sure he's out there somewhere, he may be suffering with amnesia, he may ... oh, I don't know. We can't think the worst yet but think of what you've achieved so far and will achieve, in his name. You should be proud of yourself, come back to us, when you're ready.'

I kept my emotions in check as they offered me a walking pole to replace the one I had presumably left in Viana. I promised to stay in touch and gave Mateus an extra special kiss on his head before they drove off.

Casa James was a modern barn conversion, spacious and open plan and I spent a delightful evening in the company of Nicolas's friends. However, an early night beckoned and I reluctantly bade my hosts goodnight as I needed to get back on the road the following morning and onwards to ... whatever lay ahead.

I fell asleep with Camille's last words in my head. Words of wisdom from someone so young.

✦

My next few days were varied - physically, emotionally and mentally. My short break at Casa Bonita and Casa James had bestowed me with human contact and an opportunity to put my journey into perspective but did nothing for my physical well-being. My legs ached, my backpack felt heavy and a blister required attention. The underside of my left foot was sore which caused me to walk awkwardly, throwing my weight onto my right hip. My mood began to darken, not helped by gathering rain clouds as I neared the province of Galicia, traditionally known for its varied weather.

I was not looking forward to the climb to reach O' Cebreiro. Nicolas had recommended what he called the Ruta Pradela, and after a night in a hostel in Villafranca I set off early the following morning to follow this route. I had met up with a fellow pilgrims the previous evening who suggested a shorter route but I recalled Nicolas suggesting I avoided that as it followed a busy road with noise, blind bends and fast traffic. I had bought plentiful supplies for the day ahead and after giving myself a stern talking to, set off 'with best foot forward' as Dad used to say.

I realised I had not phoned home recently and promised myself I would make contact on reaching the village at the top. The route was beautiful as it followed the River Valcarce valley, the sun had emerged which lightened my mental load and I just kept going, one foot in front of the other. A puffed 'Bon Camino' was the most I could offer as I climbed; my calf muscles regularly protesting for a stop and a massage. Many pilgrims just smiled as they leant forward on their walking sticks or poles, ever upwards. I was so thankful for my walking pole as I held on firmly to its handle, an ever-present reminder of Camille and Mateus.

I walked part way alongside a dual carriageway, meandered through chestnut woods, strode through deserted villages and hamlets and stopped for lunch by a disused barn outside Herrerias and covered the kilometres ever onwards, along earth tracks, past gorse and scrubland. A thirteen hundred metre climb may not sound much to experienced hikers but to someone in their forties for whom this Camino walking was a first, it was hard going.

'One foot in front of the other. Keep going, girl. Think of Ben. Think of Santiago.'

... And I did. The words became a familiar mantra encouraging me onwards as the climb intensified in direct proportion to my lowering energy levels. I now exchanged verbal greetings with nods and smiles.

'Only another few kilometres and you're there,' a cheery voice was directed at me as a young couple strode by.

'Wait until you're my age,' I muttered through gritted teeth.

A concrete marker announced we were now entering the region of Galicia. My spirits lifted a little, helped also by touching the ancient stone walls of Iglesia de Santa Maria la Real; a ninth-century church announcing the entrance to the hamlet of O' Cebreiro.

It was late afternoon by now and I'd been walking for ten hours. My shoulders ached, my legs ached, I was footsore and brain weary. I was also famished.

Apart from all the pilgrims, the hamlet was as if frozen in time with restored traditional thatched pallozas vying with a few more modern buildings; shops, albergues and casas offered overnight accommodation. At the third attempt I found a room for the night and my body sighed with relief as I luxuriated in a bath before changing into my light trousers, soft shoes and fleece. My blister was completely healed and the soreness under my foot lessened after adding some 'freebie' peppermint essential oil to the water. This may well have been a basic guest house but toiletries on offer were plentiful.

It had turned chilly and drizzly so I decided to find food only, phone home then retire to bed. I would feel refreshed in the morning to explore a little before setting off on my final push to meet Bryony.

I sat in bed to phone Mum, who was especially happy to hear from me, especially after she told me Dad had showed her on Google the climb to O' Cebreiro. She was most impressed! However, I really had no more to offer where Camille and Mateus were concerned and although excited to feel I now had an extension to our small family and was desperate to see Mateus again, my priority was Ben. I texted them a few photos of Mateus and promised my next call would be from Santiago. As I closed the phone it suddenly dawned on me, I was near the completion of the Walk and at that point my mood hit rock bottom. Where was Ben? I was running out of opportunities to find even the smallest hint that he was still alive. Nicolas's suggestion of Dissociative Amnesia seemed far-fetched but I still clung to that as a possibility.

Sleep would not come. Sore calves, aching left shoulder, physical tiredness, emotions, swirling thoughts both positive and negative, all conspired against me. I tossed and turned, switched the light on to write more in my diary, ate a biscuit and finally took a paracetamol in the hopes it might relax me. The next thing I knew my phone was ringing insistently.

'What the–' I grabbed it from the top of the chest of drawers alongside the bed and activated the answer button. My initial thought was it had to be Mum or Dad; although we had spoken previously who else would be phoning me at this time of night?

'Daisy? I'm sorry, it's me, Bryony,' garbled words muffled by what I presumed to be tears.

I listened through a haze of sleepiness; she'd had an accident, slipped in her hotel shower and was in hospital with a broken collar bone and bruising. Jack was on his way and had offered to sort everything out for her. She didn't need me to do anything just wanted to talk to someone. My heart went out to her as I thought of her alone in a strange hospital, in pain and unable to speak much of the language. Thank goodness Jack was close by and our conversation didn't last long after the initial details. I noticed with dismay it was 4.00am, and the thought of needing to be up and on my way within three hours selfishly occupied my thoughts. She promised she would phone if she had any difficulties that Jack couldn't sort and we confirmed Monte do Gozo to be our meeting venue. Practicalities could be sorted later.

I must have dozed off as my phone alarm suddenly broke through my sleep. Seven o'clock; I had to be on my way. Inevitably Bryony entered my thoughts as I prepared for my next stage of the walk. Bad luck had struck her again but thank goodness for Jack, at least now she was in safe hands. I hastily dressed in the same clothes as yesterday, after all who did I need to dress for apart for myself and my own comfort? Everything else I stuffed into my backpack. Neatly folding and rolling of clothes had become a thing of the past.

As I slid my phone into the front compartment, I felt paper and realised I still had a few somewhat crumpled photos of Ben. Had he stopped here? Did he even make it to here? For a short while he lay heavy on my heart but I had no answers to give. Mateus's gurgling smile suddenly appeared in front of me; so many faces, so many unexpected twists and turns to my journey. But this was not the time to dwell on what might be, I had to get on my way. I surprised myself by walking away from the main street and holding my head up high, shouted words of nothingness into the wind. Most unlike me but It worked as my stress levels subsided.

On realising I hadn't stocked up with lunch nor had I explored the hamlet I returned to a local bar where I picked up bread, cheese, fruit and water. I also showed a picture of Ben to the man serving, he could not help but agreed to put the photo in his window. I took a few photos of the stone pallozas with their peaked roofs; this evidence of a long passed simple community intrigued me. I stooped a little to enter one and marvelled at the ingenuity used to accommodate the families with their animals. I picked up a leaflet to read later and in true pilgrim style, made my backpack comfortable on my shoulders and then bent to tie my boot laces tighter. I should have done this before securing my rucksack as found myself toppling forward from the weight on my back. Various hands reached out and I felt comforted by sympathetic voices. I'd learnt my lesson and after a short rest felt ready to set off.

I had estimated seven days of walking would get me to Monte do Gozo; so close to reaching my goal of Santiago but no closer to my elusive Ben. Then, with no warning, he suddenly came into full view; I felt his arms, smelt his aftershave, heard his voice. I looked around, nothing, no-one. I stood, rooted, I had heard him, had seen him, hadn't I?

'Are you alright?'

A young man came alongside. Is that who I saw? Was my

brain playing tricks on me? Was I convincing myself of Ben's physical presence?

I nodded. 'Yes, fine,' I lied.

This mountain I had been determined to conquer was becoming my tormentor; messing with my mind but why now? Was my son trying to get through to me? It made me more determined to leave his photo where I could as I neared Santiago. He was the reason for my being here, I could not desert him now.

The Galician weather lived up to its name; drizzle became rain showers which in turn became steady downpours. At times when it ceased, I could take in the glorious views around me: vineyards, forests, hills, fields and lush pastures, I was spoilt for choice. I was looking forward to meeting up with Bryony and started to imagine spending time with her. Although quite different in character we had been at ease with each other when we spent time together in Leon and she seemed genuinely interested in my quest for answers to Ben's disappearance. For my part I was curious to find out how she and Jack were going to resolve their relationship issues. All these musings led me to think about my relationship with Shaun, marriage to divorce, intense love to the emotional chasm that had opened up. Why had it gone so wrong? Did Ben blame us? Me? His dad? How honest had he been about his emotions when I tried to explain why we could no longer live as a happy family. The words jarred, 'happy family'. It seemed so long since we had been one. Shared our home, our bed, our son, our life.

I stopped to have a drink and an apple at a water fountain in the square of a seemingly deserted village. I needed to snap out of this introspection, it wasn't doing any good, wasted energy that my body needed, not my mind. And so, with one foot in front of another, the kilometres passed. Villages and hamlets, the odd barking dog, changing landscapes but no real sign of life. So many people had abandoned these communities in search of a supposedly better livelihood to be derived from the towns.

The following day brought more torrential rain. Walking

held no pleasure. I knew each step carried me closer to Santiago but it was another low point. I stopped for lunch at a wayside cafe, enjoyed a steaming cafe con leche with a bocadillo, changed my socks and gave my waterproof a good shaking. For some reason Patrick came to mind, sporting his Marilyn Monroe T-shirt. With so much going on recently I hadn't given him a thought. Was he still here? Had he finished and returned to Ireland? Had he managed to keep off the alcohol? More importantly, just what had been his involvement with Camille and Ben? Had he told everything about the three of them and their relationships?

I felt I needed to be armed with as much information about him before I reached Santiago and whilst I was prepared for not seeing him, I harboured a wish that the three of us might meet up. After Camille he was the only person holding any clues and he just might have contact, however tenuous, with someone in the city. I was overnighting just outside Portomarin and after supper I decided there was only one way to find out Patrick's whereabouts and I used Bryony's accident as an excuse for phoning.

'Patrick, is that you?'

'For sure, and who's this young lady calling me?'

'Don't be daft, it's Daisy here.' Even if he wasn't aware, his response to my call immediately lightened my load.

'Kathleen?'

'Yes, Kathleen, Ben's mum.'

I laughed; it was such a relief to do so.

'Where are you, are you still here? What about Bryony?'

I explained my whereabouts then went on to tell him about Bryony's misfortune back in Ponferrada, how Jack had arrived and was supporting her and our intention to still meet at Monte do Gozo. I sensed from his voice he was surprised we were still on track, still putting one foot in front of another, especially as it turned out he was not far ahead of me. I'd thought he would have been further on than that but maybe he was taking it more slowly, maybe he was now savouring the journey, allowing himself time to assimilate his thoughts and enjoy his surroundings. Maybe some fact might get triggered where Camille, Ben and he was concerned.

So bound up with sharing Bryony's misfortune I was then a little disappointed by his casual comments when I told him about meeting Camille and Mateus at Casa Bonita. He was happy for me, didn't seem surprised and said he looked forward to sharing 'all news' hopefully in Santiago.

'So, we're all still on track, I'll keep a look out for you two Kathleens. One with a crutch, the other struggling to support.'

'Patrick! It's her shoulder, not her leg, you're not listening.'

He laughed. 'Chill, Daisy. We'll all make it. We'll raise a glass or two to our success, just like Burgos, and to Ben – I haven't forgotten him.'

He didn't elaborate.

'Give me a ring if you need anything, we'll meet again.'

I smiled as Vera Lynn came to mind. He'd probably never heard of her.

I felt reassured on making contact with him and hearing his voice. With so much emotion behind me, and the physical end in sight, I seemed to be experiencing a heightened conflict between positivity and negativity. The current loneliness of my daily solo walking with the excitement of reaching Santiago. This could well be my last opportunity to find out anything or at the worst, nothing, about Ben. The sheer thought of that caused an uneasy fluttering in my stomach. Dad had frequently reminded me about that possibility but I was still not completely prepared to accept a negative conclusion. There had to be an answer somewhere and I was determined to find it.

The number of pilgrims along the way was increasing as we all sought our respective end goals. The Galician weather continued to accompany us and the walking was muddy underfoot and wet overhead. I stopped overnight at Palais de Rei, a small enough town but there was nothing to draw me to explore. Under different circumstances I might well have rested awhile but I was itching to get to Monte do Gozo and with that in mind phoning Bryony was paramount.

'Where are you?' came her first question.

'Where are you?' came my reply.

Only sixty kilometres separated us; she was in Santiago! She sounded buoyant. She had two rooms booked and her collar bone was healing.

'Monte do Gozo here we come. I'll be wearing the pink carnation! See you in three days, d'you reckon?' She sounded excited at the thought of us being together again and her positivity had an effect off on me. I – we – were there, nearly there. Journey's end, physically at least.

Three days, I could easily do that. I longed to give her a hug and get one in return, I craved physical human contact, the touch, the feel of another person. If it couldn't be Ben, then Bryony would do!

I wondered about the situation between her and Jack, two rooms, I noticed two rooms were mentioned. Was he still there? Had he left? So many questions.

Part 3, Leon to Santiago

11

Patrick

CAMILLE LEFT SOON after she had delivered her words of wisdom, and this time I knew we would meet again, sometime, somewhere. I promised I would stay in touch, indeed wanted to re-establish our relationship – platonic of course. She was always easy to talk to when the three of us were together, probably easier than it was to talk to Ben. She had encouraged confidences and I have to admit I felt a bit like a small child listening to her. She had given me a lot to think about as I had with her and ... thinking required a drink, only one I vowed to myself.

There was still a warmth to the late afternoon sun and the street hustle and bustle relaxed me. I was happy to be alone with my thoughts. Pilgrims passed by, limping, striding, ambling, chatting. Some were hunched by the weight of their backpacks, others dressed for a day of relaxation. I searched their faces but did not recognise any familiar drinking partners and then idly wondered where the two 'girls' might be. Were they together? Or solo walking? Had they already moved on or not even arrived?

As I sat, one drink became two, two drinks became three, then four as the empty bottles accumulated on the table. I was sufficiently aware of what I was doing but not strong enough to call 'last orders'. Thoughts, so many thoughts – good, bad and indifferent – became muddled and I knew I had to find a quiet place in which to lie down and allow sleep to wash over me, purge my returned weakness for the booze. I couldn't remember my way back to my room so wandered the alleys until I found a quiet and shaded park ... yet again!

It didn't work; images of Mam, Gran, my absent dad (somewhat vague) Ben, Camille, Mateus – even the two girls – swirled and invaded. In any other circumstances I would have welcomed them, now all I wanted was the opportunity to blank everything out until my brain was ready to function again.

I awoke to the tolling of a church bell: 10.00pm. Bloody hell, I'd done it again. Would the hostel door still be open? I couldn't make up my mind whether to go in search of food, stay put or find my room and get organised. An element of practicality took over as I decided it would be better to prepare to get on the road in the morning; if an open cafe could provide a takeaway snack so much the better. Groggily, not only did I find a cafe I also found my way back to the old quarter of the city and my room. Ahead, the outline of the cathedral beckoned and I promised myself a quick visit in the morning to light a candle, as I had done in Burgos. Santiago then beckoned, by my reckoning roughly 180 kilometres away. Hopefully I would cover it in about ten days; no solid reason to do so, apart from Ben of course, just my intention.

✦

Seven o'clock the next morning, found me heading for the cathedral, only to find it didn't open until 9.30.

'Mierda, mierda.'

I knocked at the solid front door as if it might, by magic or spiritual intervention, open up.

'Apologies, Santa Maria.'

For some reason Gran's face suddenly came into view. An image of her moving from the kitchen sink of soap suds to slap me behind my knees when, as a child I swore in front of her.

'Apologies, Gran.'

I was in a quandary. To wait two and a half hours in order to light a candle, say a prayer or whatever or head off on the final stage. Yesterday's conversation with Camille came to

170

mind, might there be two lads in Santiago who could throw a light on Ben's disappearance? If there was, I needed to find them. Opportunities were gradually running out. I sat on a bench noticing I wasn't the only early bird as two snoring pilgrims caught my eye – worn boots positioned under the seats with a couple of bottles tucked into them and backpacks used as pillows. That might have been me two years ago, how many times had I regularly crashed out on a bench unable to find my way to my hostel?

'Say a prayer for your old gran, and ye mam and get on your way.'

Why was it that suddenly Gran was entering my life so vividly? Was she trying to tell me something? Is she OK? Is Mam OK?

I did as Gran bid, picked up my backpack, gave a 'Bon Camino' to the slumbering walkers and went to the impressively carved front entrance to the cathedral, where I stood and quietly said a prayer. The first for many a year. I felt compelled to run my hand over the ornate carving and as I traced the shapes, I felt rather than saw the pathway my life had taken. At times smooth but mainly bumpy and with no direction. Suddenly the reason for my coming to Northern Spain again fell into place. It wasn't just my absent dad, my wastrel of a mum. It wasn't just the need to fill my empty days, or turn my back on my wasted life. Something deeper was stirring – there were good people out there who needed me – and I needed them.

'Shit, man, you're getting philosophical in your old age. These ladies have obviously been sent to sort you out, to give you a purpose in life. So, get on with it.'

I was speaking aloud but my dormant fellow pilgrims remained comatose. I briefly wondered the life story behind them, they looked like I had so frequently felt when undertaking my first Camino. Had others looked upon me as I was now looking upon them? A groan from one brought me back to the present. I was avoiding that first step along the final Camino stage, to achieve perhaps the most useful part of my life so far, why was I stalling? Father Dickinson then came to mind, I could see him standing outside St Joseph's with me as a youngster alongside him and here he was now, pointing a finger in the direction of Santiago, it was time to leave.

As I set off following the brass arrow markers set in the ground, I also sensed within me an element of worry. What happens if the city does not throw up the answers we all hoped for? Then what?

There was only one way to find out ...

I jogged and walked my way through the landscape beyond Leon. It was a quiet stage both in the number of pilgrims, which surprised me, and the countryside itself. It was also quite easy underfoot so I made good progress, channeling all my energy into the journey; stopping only to eat and catch my breath. Villages came and went, some appeared abandoned, others in various stages of repair. Two days without an alcoholic drink became three, then four, I was back on track, in more senses than one. Various faces accompanied me, coming and going at will, all seemingly encouraging me to keep going. Sleep became instantaneous and recuperative, each morning found me revived and eager to set off.

'Patrick?'

My phone had rung persistently until I chose to answer it. Truth be told I wanted no interruption, keen as I was to concentrate on the path ahead. Santiago was drawing ever closer but there were still many kilometres to cover, including up and over the mountains appearing on the horizon.

'Patrick? She's left, she came back like we thought, Daisy I mean. Oh God, Patrick I would have loved for you to have been here. I've now got a sort of mother-in-law, Mateus has got another granny.' The excitement within her voice was unmistakable.

'Hang on a minute, Cam ...'

I removed my backpack and sat with my back against the remains of a wall, the stones were warm to my touch but strangely I was not relaxed.

'Fuck, fuck, fuck.'

'What are you saying?'

I paused and took a swig of water before I replied.

'Camille, that's great.'

No, it wasn't, my heart was racing, envy of her happiness was bubbling up within me. Why for God's sake?

'That's great, Cam ...'

'I hope you don't mind; she came back to Bonita like we thought she might, she's left now, we took her to Astorga, her aim is still to reach Santiago. I gave her your phone number, you don't mind, do you? She wanted to be able to get in touch if she finds out anything. You've got hers, haven't you?'

Have I? I didn't think so.

Questions, statements, details. Words tumbled over each other as she told me about Daisy's visit. She didn't stop but my mind was elsewhere. Everyone around me has someone to turn to, who do I bloody have? Or what do I have? Memories of a crap life, that's about the sum of it.

'Patrick, are you there?'

I tried to concentrate. I was happy for Daisy to have my number. Yes, I'm sure the pair of us would bump into each other in Santiago. Yes, I will stay in touch with you, and so on.

'I must get on, Cam, I've got to find a bed for the night. Yeh, I know that sounds a bit organised for me ... I'm aiming for Rabanal.'

I sat as confused thoughts of my earlier life surfaced again. Memories of my short friendship with Peter back in County Antrim when we were kids, when his mum took me in, his house, his bedroom, the meals they ate, the warmth of the place. Mum made little effort, too busy as she was with whichever man was current, and Gran, bless her, tried her hardest but came a poor second. Father Dickinson even flashed into my mind again, without that conversation with him I wouldn't even be here, leaning against this stone wall, listening to someone who – God damn it – could have been the mother of my child. I continued sitting whilst chewing on a squashed protein bar I had found lurking in a pocket. I allowed myself a bit longer in which to wallow, cursed my family, cursed my absent dad, cursed my lack of direction – in fact, cursed the whole bloody world ... and felt better for it.

Positivity returned, maybe this walk was to be the turning point in my life, God knows how long it's taken to inject some semblance of normality into my everyday being. God – and I – know it's been long enough. Small steps, that's what. I had the friendship of Camille, well sort of. I possibly had Daisy to get to know better, more through our shared quest. Bryony lurked on the outside, it would be good to find out how she was faring, and of course Ben was the common denominator. Gran and Mum I put into a separate box for now. My relationship with them had to be addressed at some point.

Mentally I was taking these small steps but physically I was striding out. The weather was beginning to change as low cloud and drizzle replaced the earlier blue sky and warm sunshine that had dominated most of the journey, but this was of little consequence to me. What will be, will be.

Rabanal, small towns, villages, hamlets, fields, woodlands and some road walking came and went. Places travelled through triggered memories of my first Camino walk, alone or temporarily shared with other pilgrims, sometimes sober, sometimes less so. The kilometres passed but no call from Daisy. I wasn't concerned, indeed maybe I had read too much into Camille's phone call. No news is good news I kept telling myself. I reached Villafranca which I remembered well, I had been walking with someone at the time but it was a dim and distant memory. I recognised the streets and the Plaza Mayor where I had shared a drink or two.

I overnighted in a basic albergue and shared a communal pilgrim supper of chicken and vegetables, chunks of rustic bread washed down with a strong but palatable red wine – just the one glass. I felt more like a pilgrim than I had done for a while as I shared experiences with others at my table. I kept my details sparse, being more of a listener than a talker. A Norwegian lass caught my interest as she regaled us with her 'Camino Adventure' as she called it, from parting with her girlfriend near Burgos (as a walking partner, she explained) to spending time with Jacques (whoever he was) for 'three wonderful days and nights (no more detail given). Burgos must have an effect on relationships, I idly thought but chose to keep shtum. I also decided against introducing myself to her, I had enough on my plate and anyway, decided I didn't want to end up as one her trophies.

I turned in early, knowing the following day was going to be one of the most strenuous along the Camino; up and over the pass into O' Cebreiro and onwards through Galicia, home to Santiago de Compostela – and who knows what? I found it difficult to sleep; Ben's face flashed into my mind, Camille, Gran, me as a kid, me being an embarrassment to others as drink had accompanied me. I lay on a bottom bunk in the dormitory, trying to ignore snoring, farting, other restless bodies, including the one above me, as I consciously relaxed my tired limbs, trying hard to blank out my swirling thoughts.

O'Cebreiro was hard work, especially as the drizzle intensified. I climbed with a steady pace, ignoring my protesting muscles and a slight rub of the rucksack on my shoulder. The village was overrun with pilgrims poking and peering into the ancient pallozas. I bought a snack and a bottle of water and did a quick walk around the village, imagining the life villagers must have led all those years ago, and continued on my way. Downhill was pretty hard-going, Galicia's rain was soft and insistent but I was ready for a damp spell. My cape bore the brunt of the downpours and I was glad I had chosen a cape over a waterproof, not least for the fact not only did I remain dry under it so did my rucksack.

I know it's a given fact that walking through woods – or walking anywhere – is good for your mental well-being and that day was no exception. I was alone (which suits me), in strong health (a realisation that drink is not the answer to all life's ails) and in good spirits. The eucalyptus trees dripped on me from overhead as wet leaves and a muddy, uneven track squelched underfoot but I strode onwards, thankful my leg muscles had stopped aching.

Going downhill was starting to get a bit tough as uneven boulders hidden beneath the fallen, soggy leaves threatened to turn my ankle. Nothing risky, just the need to take care and I realised trainers were now not the best footwear. As I stopped to undo my walking boots tied to the rucksack strap, my phone vibrated but by the time I had done a pocket search the caller had given up. For ease I put it in my shorts' pocket, just in case.

Wrong number, I decided.

It was strange how my phone had lay dormant for much of the walk but on nearing Santiago started to spring to life. As I was thinking of others so it seemed others were thinking of me. I even found myself idly wondering whether St James had a part to play in this, was his presence subconsciously strengthening my very being with each step?

'Bloody hell, not again.'

My phone was vibrating.

'Patrick, is that you, son?'

'Gran?'

'Course it is, who did ye think it bloody was, Mary Mother of Jesus?'

I grinned, actually I laughed aloud.

'Hold on, Gran, don't go away, I'm needing to stop properly. Stay there, d'you understand?'

'I may be old, son, but I'm not senile, though how that's come about I don't know. I'm surrounded by doddering old farts.'

I resisted asking whether she counted Mum amongst these 'farts' (always a favourite word of hers). I also realised my heart was pounding. Why was she phoning?'

'OK, Gran, I don't believe it. First, how are you?'

As ever she deflected the question from herself.

'It's Father Dickinson, y'know? He died – last week.'

I realised I had been holding my breath as I gave a sudden exhale.

'How?'

'Heart, he'd been ill for a while but no-one expected this.'

'I'm so sorry, Gran.'

'Why are you saying that to me?'

'Well, he'd been kind to us, hadn't he?'

176

She didn't answer, actually, she did but with an inconsequential detail about how she'd heard the news.

'He helped set you on a better path, didn't he?'

Gran's conversations never flowed, had always lurched from subject to subject without time to respond, as if her thought processes overrode each other and that last statement was loaded, even if she hadn't realised.

'He was buried yesterday.'

I was relieved. I didn't have to make a decision about returning.

'How's Mum?' There. I'd done it. One of us had to make the first move.

Silence.

'She's actually pretty fine, for ye mum, that is.'

'Does she mention me?'

'Yes. I know Father only died a week ago but she's sort of … gone quiet, as if she's … reflecting. Is that the right word? Talking about you.'

I wanted to give her a hug as I felt a welling up of emotion.

'Yes, Gran, that's absolutely the right word. Why is she talking about me?'

'You are her son.'

I let that pass.

'Shall I phone her?'

'In your own time. She's not going anywhere.'

Gran gave me Mum's number and I promised I'd phone once I reached Santiago.

'Thanks, Gran. Thank you for phoning.' I then heard myself uttering words not used for so many years.

'I love you, thank you.' I clutched the phone and I cried – properly, tears fell, man tears, I gulped but allowed them to fall unchecked, it was as if years of pent-up emotions were desperate to be shed. No-one passed by but it wouldn't have disturbed or embarrassed me, such was my need for release.

I eventually drank from my water bottle and chewed on a muesli bar as I processed all Gran had told me. Maybe I was now beginning to have a reason to return – maybe even settle for a while. If possible, sort my relationship with Mum and give Gran a huge hug. Even if I didn't stay, I would make it up, get my life back on an even keel. But first, I still had unfinished business here.

Bryony and Daisy, they appeared to be in touch with each other, no worries there. To meet them in Santiago, that would be my aim. Ben then entered my thoughts. I was completely at a loss where he was concerned. Was he alive? Was he in this country? Moved away? Was he dead? If so, how? Where? How could I help Daisy complete her quest? Camille had mentioned the two friends from a while ago, maybe a lead there. I realised arrival in Santiago might well be the end of my physical journey but not the mental or emotional one.

The afternoon wore on and I recalled from my first time here a small town called Portomarin was not far away and decided to aim for that over the next couple of days. Meanwhile, basic hostels would be fine. The yellow arrows kept me on track as I continued through woodlands and quiet country roads. With the rain lessening and blue sky appearing, not to mention phone calls received, my mood was light. I realised I was no different from others; I did need people, contrary to what I had kept telling myself. Opportunities for solitude should be experienced but at the end of the day, as humans we need human contact. I jogged past a few pilgrims with a cheery 'Bon Camino' and walked with a German guy for a while. Like me he was on his second journey; it was good to talk but I felt I was initiating the conversation as monosyllabic answers came back each time. I sensed he was at one with nature and his own company so bade him farewell, suggesting we might meet in Portomarin. At least I had given him the opportunity if he wished to take it up.

Portomarin had fascinated me last time; a village moved peace-meal to its current position on higher ground when the nearby river was dammed to create a reservoir. It reminded me of a similar situation back home when the River Liffey was dammed, flooding local cottages, to create a reservoir whose name I can never remember. I do recall we did a school outing to it as part of a geography field trip, at least my year group did, I bunked off as was my wont in those troubled days. I decided to spend a bit of time in the village as much to dry off my boots and rucksack as re-acquaint myself with its history. My 'repellent' waterproof cape dripped everywhere and had started to let in water at the seams so my shirt and shorts were also sopping. I needed to sort myself out. I also felt weary and had to acknowledge I had pushed myself physically over the preceding kilometres.

It was still daylight when I arrived. I treated myself to a single room above a bar; there was plenty of hot water so I washed my T-shirt, socks and a pair of pants, all of which were long overdue, and hung everything around the place to dry and after a quick meal in the bar downstairs – one drink only – I turned in. I slept well, so well in fact that the sun was streaming through the window and to my horror I saw it was mid-morning.

To add to the confusion my phone started sounding off under my pillow, this was all getting too much. A frantic sounding Daisy garbled words of apology.

'I'm sorry Patrick, it's me, Daisy, remember me? Ben's mum. Camille did tell you, didn't she? I didn't know who else to phone. It's Bryony.'

I listened as words tumbled; a fall in the shower, broken collarbone, taken to hospital near Ponferrada, which I reckoned was a bit before O'Cebreiro. She was OK. Daisy continued gabbling and I felt it was her who needed the support. By the time she had finished it appeared the latest situation to have befallen Bryony had already been sorted. Bryony? Was she accident prone or a bit of a drama queen? Either way it appears Jack, her husband, was on his way to see her; what input he'd give Daisy didn't know, suffice to say the girls were aiming eventually to reach Santiago together.

She hardly drew breath as she continued. She was still on the search for Ben, which of course was the reason for her being here and, more importantly, she was trying hard to prepare herself for a negative as much as a positive outcome. She excitedly talked about how she had met Mateus and Camille and how having them in her life was giving her the impetus to continue the search ... and so on and so on. I finally got a word in.

'OK, is there anything I can do? Where are you?'

Turns out she was not that far behind me which was surprising until I acknowledged to myself the countless reasons and number of times I had pressed the pause button within my journey.

She didn't want anything from me except know I was at the end of the phone and that hopefully we would all meet up in Santiago.

'Sounds a good idea, stay in touch. I'm here, well, here enough to help if you or Bryony need anything.'

The relief in her voice spoke volumes and I was touched to think my last words had helped, though to be honest I wasn't sure what I could do.

'Thank you, Patrick. You're a brick.'

I grinned to myself as I deliberately chose to misinterpret her last word.

A pr---, that was something I had been, on many occasions in my life. A word used frequently by me as a teenager in response to other kids as we insulted each other, goading each into landing the first blow.

Gran's face stared out at me as I saw myself come into her kitchen with a bloody nose or cut lip. The shrug of her shoulders as she handed me a cloth, all the time muttering under her breath. The memory reinforced my need to contact Mum and I promised myself and Gran I would, soon.

The day in Portomarin was being eaten into by unforeseen circumstances but I was still keen to explore this village. Not often had I taken time out to savour the journey and today I was determined to stick to my plan. I could still find the next hostel before darkness fell. I walked around the church marvelling that it had been saved from the flooding by being moved stone by stone from its original position. Remains of blown-up houses and the old stone bridge gave testimony to the detailed planning that must have gone into this massive project of the 60s. It really impressed me and I promised myself a visit to the River Liffey project when I returned home.

When I finally set off, I walked with confidence, aware of the gathering numbers of pilgrims pacing out through the eucalyptus woods. After two days of solid walking, I finally made it onto an asphalt road, past the airport, towards Monte do Gozo. It was manic after the quiet of the Galician countryside. Coach loads of people were arriving to experience one day's walking into the city. Food vans were everywhere, empty cans and cartons littered the ground. Genuine pilgrims could be identified by weary but smiling faces, untidy hair, heavy rucksacks and worn walking boots, whilst the day trippers came with shopping bags, tidy trousers and shoes; not a muddy waterproof in sight.

I decided to stay in the albergue overnight, to reach Santiago in time for the midday service the next day. The memory of Father Dickinson had accompanied me these past kilometres and the desire to offer up a prayer was strangely overwhelming; when all's said and done, he was the one who inspired me to undertake this journey. I recalled that to reach the cathedral and find a seat required an early start and nimble feet. Queues outside it built up from early morning and many pilgrims were unlucky. There was always tomorrow but for me it was important, on many levels, to experience the service on the day.

And I did. I didn't understand a word as Spanish was the language but that was inconsequential. I sat between a Canadian girl and a Swedish guy; many miles separated our countries but we were united by a common achievement. I swear I could sense emotions linking us. I felt different from last time, for a start I was sober, I had companions to look out for and, more importantly, unfinished tasks to pursue. Unable to follow the service word for word, I was free to take in my surroundings. The place was packed: pilgrims and tourists, old, young, clean, bedraggled, smiling, sombre; apart from the incantations you could have heard a pin drop. The sympathetically lit high altar drew me in. A statue I assumed to be St James was surrounded by others unknown to me. The impressive, ornate incense burner was hanging from the roof and I wondered whether today would be my lucky day. I didn't see the spectacle surrounding its use last time and as the service continued, I was to remain disappointed. Suddenly, Daisy came into my mind – and Ben. I hoped to bump into her and Bryony and maybe visit the cathedral again in their company. Ben? Might he be here? Or passed through? Be remembered by anyone we might speak to?

After grabbing a bocadillo I sat in the Praza do Obradoiro, the main square where pilgrims traditionally congregate. Relaxed in the sunshine, I people watched. Some sat alone as I did, others in pairs and groups. Voices and laughter filled the air giving an atmosphere of achievement. I have to admit to a sense of – not loneliness exactly, more like aloneness. I decided to head for the Pilgrims Office to claim the Compostela, the certificate of achievement awarded to all who have covered at least the final one hundred kilometres. Although I had collected one two years ago, I'm not sure what happened to it. I don't recall ever having seen it; the chances are it never even arrived with me back in Ireland. Today, that incident spoke volumes, I had not been worthy of it. As I stood in the queue, I idly questioned to myself whether the certificate should be awarded to those who only covered this last part of the Camino, considering the hardship experienced by the likes of us who have travelled the whole journey, but didn't like to ask how that came about.

It was at that point I noticed a message board covered with scraps of paper. Messages left, questions asked, answers given. Ben flashed into my mind, here was the obvious place to localise the quest for him. I hastily scribbled as words formed in my mind, someone, somewhere must have heard, through a friend, a friend of a friend, anyone, anything connected to him. I knew that not everyone returns home, some stay, find work, meet others, continue with their wanderings. Among them might be hidden a clue to his disappearance. As I signed off with my name and mobile number, Daisy came to mind, I really hoped to meet her and share her search within Santiago.

I half wanted to ring her but resisted, I had her number should the need arise.

I found a cheap hostel and to begin with booked in for one night, I was also allowed to leave my backpack on a bunk bed. I decided to celebrate my arrival with one drink and find something to eat. Without warning my aloneness manifested itself again, Santiago was the climax of the journey but not the best place after many days of solo travelling. The city was buzzing but I was not part of it. I sat outside a bar in the late afternoon sun and watched the busy world go by. I was feeling disconnected, another drink seemed the answer.

'Señor, pleez, time to go.' A shaking of my shoulder awoke me. I felt dreadful, dry-mouth, nasty taste, heavy head. I was slumped over, having half fallen from the chair. One or two people walked round me, no-one stopped to speak or check I was OK.

How I made it back to the hostel I do not know. Then of course, lock out had occurred. I couldn't get in. I sunk to the ground outside the front door.

'Heh mate, what the bloody hell ... you look crap.'

I felt crap as I looked up.

'You're one lucky guy it was me who came along. No time for questions, let's get you in.'

The next thing I knew I was in a simple room lying on a single bed.

'Questions in the morning,' and that was that.

✦

I awoke to voices outside my door. Through the window, dawn was breaking. I was used to early risers, the sound as people clambered from bunks, backpacks being reassembled, whispering, to-ing and fro-ing to the showers. But this was Santiago, the end of the line, goal achieved. So why such early voices? I lay, gathering my thoughts, recalling last night. Embarrassment flooded my brain when I realised what I had done and, what was worse, I had drunk alone. A knock at the door brought me back to where I was.

'When you're ready come to the office, I'll be there, come and have a coffee.'

Five minutes under a cold shower (no hot water left) and I felt rejuvenated. Clean clothes from my rucksack and I felt almost normal.

'Morning, have a coffee. I'm Phil. Pedro runs the place but I cover when he's away.'

I took the mug and sat at the desk opposite Phil. Paperwork was strewn everywhere. A large box of assorted walking clothing was under the window. Maps were pinned to the walls and leaflets in wire trays filled spaces in between.

'Morning, I'm Patrick, I've just arrived. I feel shit. Thanks for last night.'

'I've been there, I know the feeling.' Phillip shook my hand and smiled, putting me at my ease, he did not offer further details.

'It's a long story,' I replied.

'I'm not going anywhere – for a while.'

I felt a sudden need to confide, unburden, call it what you may, but decided my distant past was too complicated and irrelevant to dwell upon in front of a completely unknown but welcoming stranger, and so concentrated on the two Kathleens (as I called them). Coming from Australia, Phil looked puzzled and I had to explain to him the reason why I called them that which completely diluted any humour. He showed more interest in Ben's story and suggested we meet up later after he had completed his tasks. He gave me the name of a bar, booked me into the hostel for another couple of nights and agreed I could leave my possessions in the office.

I ordered a cafe negro and sat with my phone on the table. My head felt clearer and my mind more alert. Today I had to phone Mum, later though.

'Penny for them?' A chair was scraped on the ground as Phil sat down. Two coffees ordered and I found myself explaining in greater detail about Daisy and Ben. Certain facts about my relationship with Ben I omitted or glossed over. I did mention our fight and Ben's possible state of mind and mentioned Camille in passing but didn't feel it important to the search.

'If anywhere, here surely must throw up a clue, if it exists.'

'Have you seen the noticeboard in the Pilgrims Office? You could leave a message there.'

I explained I had already done that.

'I'll make a few enquiries and ask Pedro, he knows everyone. There's some English guys who hang out in a bar not far from here. Non returnees they call themselves! I'll introduce you if you like. I'm sure they won't hold it against you, being Irish!'

I liked his sense of humour.

✦

I spent the following two days behaving myself. One drink allowed each evening, then it was sparkling water. I was introduced to Pedro who introduced me to the English guys but Ben's name rang no bells. The only possibility they could offer was someone called Jonno who worked in a bar on the way to Finisterre, another English guy who was expected back to Santiago after visiting his folks. Pedro had also spoken to the manager of another hostel in the city to see if he had any ideas, but no luck. I felt really pissed off and angry that Ben could disappear with no leads to follow. What had he been playing at? Why? I really wanted to believe he was still alive but I – we – had to face the possibility ... I couldn't even put the thought into words. How could little Mateus grow up never knowing his father? The irony was not lost on me. Whilst wanting to reunite with Daisy and Bryony, however briefly, I also worried about how Daisy would cope. It seemed as if she might have to return home none the wiser – except for Camille and Mateus of course.

Thinking of Daisy and Ben jogged my mind about Mum. Was I putting off making contact? I know Gran had said all was fine but was she coating a bitter pill with her choice of words? I needed to hear Mum's voice and, more importantly, hear what she might have to say to me, after all I was her son. If I was going to make the effort to make contact, the least she could do was respond. My unknown father came to mind again, I hadn't given him much thought recently; perhaps she might be prepared to throw some light on his whereabouts, if indeed it was known.

During the second afternoon, I meandered through the narrow streets and found myself in a park overlooking the cathedral. Couples walked arm in arm, elderly men sat and shared a conversation, children scooted past. A few good-looking lasses caught my eye, all were occupied, sharing the warmth of the day, reinforcing yet again my solitary status. I sat on a bench a little further down from a long-bearded gentleman who was sitting, legs crossed, arms folded in contemplation; a life-sized sculpture of the famous Spanish dramatist Ramón Maria del Valle-Inclán who had spent his early years in Santiago de Compostela (as I found out later). I folded my arms, then my legs, realised what I was doing and hastily unfolded them.

Daisy and Bryony came to mind again. We all shared a common goal, each goal centred around one person, we were all here, journeying towards a resolution in our lives and the foundation of mine was a phone number away. I tapped in the number; it took what seemed like eternity to be answered.

'Mam?'

'Patrick? Is that you, son?'

'It is.'

'Ye gran said–'

'I know.'

Silence.

'How are ye, son?'

'Fine.'

'Where are you?'

That question gave me permission to elaborate a little more as I explained about my return Camino journey. I kept it brief, the purpose of the call was to make contact not resolve our relationship, that could come later, face to face, if it was to be.

I mentioned Father Dickinson and hesitantly raised the subject of my dad. Mum was not much help where he was concerned, at least, professed not to have any worthwhile details. When I suggested he might have come from Northern Spain she clammed up a little and then hotly denied the fact. Was it embarrassment or disinterest? Having had so little interaction with her over the years, I had no way of recognising clues from her voice or how she expressed herself.

I let it drop.

It was decidedly strained between us. I sensed she was not going to open up or apologise or anything for that matter. The important thing was, we had spoken and I was satisfied with that for now.

'Will ye phone me when ye come home, if you're coming back that is.'

I deliberately remained non-committal. There was too much hurt within me, too much muddy water flowing under the bridge to immediately accede to her request.

'Good bye, son. Please stay in touch.'

I sat and my mind went back to the Ireland of my childhood. What shit I had endured. So many wasted years, with my education, my relationships, my stability, my emotions, my lack of social integration. However, what with the Ben thing and meeting his mum, this journey had started to turn me into a man, a man of worth, with confidence in my ability to survive, relate to others, think positively about the future, my future.

'Patrick? Patrick...?' Female shouting brought me back down to earth.

'Ye Gods! My Kathleens, Daisy? Bryony?'

There they were, stepping towards me, one carefully holding her shoulder the other rushing to greet me.

I'm not ashamed to admit I shed a few tears, again. Daisy cried; Bryony cried. I stood up, we hugged, we held onto each other.

'Shit, man, this is like Burgos all over again,' I finally spoke as we hung onto each other.

'You look more of a mess though,' Bryony grinned as she finally broke our emotional statue.

'Give me time,' I finally responded. 'I just need a bit of time, nothing major, just need time to myself. I'll explain, I'll explain all ... and hear what you've been up to ...' I looked questioningly at Bryony's arm as I spoke.

As much as I wanted to hear their news and share mine, I needed to be alone, to process my conversation with Mum. I felt a little guilty keeping back from Daisy the information regarding the English guy Jonno, but justified it as fairly insignificant at the moment, as until I had met him there was nothing to say.

'Bear with me.'

I gave them the name of a bar and we agreed to meet for breakfast next morning. Then, for some obscure reason, Father Dickinson came to mind. Was he having a hand in all this again? Was it his hand rather than the hand of St James guiding us? I backed off from any more spiritual meanderings, this was just not me, at least, not the old me.

12

Daisy and Bryony meet at Gozo and Onwards to Santiago

'WE'VE DONE IT – Daisy- I'm over here.' Bryony held her arm as she stepped from the taxi.

Daisy waved excitedly as she heard Bryony's voice. She balanced her rucksack over one shoulder and pushed her way through a group of elderly ladies who looked as if they were on a day out. The two friends laughed and hugged each other, Daisy carefully acknowledging the sling supporting her friend's arm.

'You've lost weight,' Bryony commented.

'You look as if you've been pampering yourself,' returned Daisy.

'Let's move away from the crowd.' Bryony began to walk to where the visitors thinned out.

As expected, Monte do Gozo was busy with pilgrims, coach parties, day trippers and temporary pilgrims who arrived in time to leave and walk the final kilometres into Santiago. Burger vans, sandwich vans, litter and all the hustle and bustle associated with a popular landmark completed the picture. The two girls chatted superficially and took each other's photos as they stopped under the huge stone monument commemorating Pope John Paul's visit in the 1980s.

'It's a bit disappointing,' commented Daisy. 'I can't see the cathedral, it's all eucalyptus and buildings. I thought the statue was of two pilgrims pointing towards the spires, I'm sure that's what my guidebook says.'

Bryony laughed. 'Just enjoy it, we're here, we've made it.'

Daisy was correct in her assertion and had they walked a short distance away from the stone monument they would have come across the bronze pilgrim statue.

'We've all made it.' The two friends looked round.

A young girl stood by them looking weary but ecstatic of voice, she was fumbling with her phone and Daisy offered to take her photo in front of the statue. She explained she had originally flown from Canada with the aim of walking the Camino from St Jean Pied de Port in forty days, this was perfectly doable but it had taken her fifty days in the end. As with so many, once she had started, she realised the import-ance and necessity to stop and recharge mentally, emotionally and physically and her thoughtful boss back home had allowed her unpaid leave in order to complete. She sounded appreciative of having others to talk to and Daisy and Bryony seemed happy to listen and in return, briefly but selectively told her about their respective journeys; testing emotions, blisters, broken bones, families left behind.

'… And that's just for starters,' Bryony breezily commented.

They bade farewell as the young girl explained her need to get going; unlike them, her time in Santiago was limited by her flight home.

Daisy was by now very excited to share all her news and both were bubbling with the realisation they had accom-plished their goal – bar any unforeseen accident. They bought two unappetizing burgers with a polystyrene mug of luke-warm coffee and found a space to sit among all the visiting pilgrims – genuine and not. Photos of Mateus and Camille were shared as Daisy explained her meeting them for the first time. She then took a photo of Ben from her rucksack.

'I want him to see the last final kilometres, I want him to be alongside me as I finish … as we finish. He'll be my guide … wherever.' She shrugged her shoulders as if to acknowledge there may still be an unresolved conclusion to her search.

Bryony looked at her watch.

'Oh, I'm sorry, I'm sorry, I'm gabbling on.'

Bryony nudged her affectionately. '… And so you should.'

They agreed all further news to be shared on arrival, found an overflowing bin for their empty cartons and set off for the last short stage into the city. They were surrounded by all manner of walkers; old folk, younger ones, some fleet of foot, others wearily plodding, some with shopping bags, other with backpacks, all with the same goal.

The walk into Santiago is an uninspiring one. The flat concrete paving underfoot – a world away from the terrains covered over passed kilometres – can make for a disheartening final leg of the journey. The sounds of traffic, the pollution from vehicle fumes or the rumble of a passing train can blanket any feeling of achievement and so it was for the two girls as they walked side by side with Galician drizzle falling from an overcast sky. Daisy kept an ever-watchful eye over Bryony who periodically delved beneath her waterproof to straighten her sling.

'You're very subdued.' It was Daisy who finally broke the silence.

'It's all a bit of an anti-climax, like being back at home heading for the city centre.'

'What, dressed like this? I can't imagine you making for the shops in muddy boots and a mac,' Daisy replied as she hoisted her backpack into a more comfortable position. 'Don't let negativity spoil this day, the rain will stop and we'll be there very soon, maybe even make it into the cathedral. Then we can stop, I can take off my boots and we'll celebrate.'

'You've not mentioned Ben since Gozo…' Bryony hesitated.

Daisy filled the silence between them. She pulled Ben's photo from her pocket.

'Like I said, he is with me, let's just get there. I want to climb those steps with him close by. I want to kneel, send a prayer, phone Mum and Dad. Then we'll celebrate – and talk. Hang on a minute though, I want to get my shell out and tie it on my backpack before we enter. Have you got yours?'

Bryony shook her head.

'It's in my rucksack in the hotel. I didn't think about it. Damn and blast.' As she spoke her phone rang. She took one look at the screen and closed it down. 'Jack, he can wait. I'll be back home before too long – discussions, and decisions, then.'

'Dare I ask?'

'No, not at the moment. Let's not spoil this by discussing my marital problems. D'you think we'll bump into Patrick? D'you think he'll be wearing his Marilyn Monroe T-shirt?'

It was as if she was trying to deflect conversation – and it worked as they both laughed at the image.

The cathedral spires soared to the cloudy skies ahead of them as they took the Rua de St Pedro and finally the Porto do Camino – Gate of the Way – into the old city. A man wearing traditional costume with a tall black cap, stood playing his Spanish bagpipes, a cheerful and evocative rendition as if to welcome the two friends to his city.

And there they finally stood on the outskirts of the medieval square. They had arrived, achieved their goal and were speechless. Bryony looked towards her friend, tears running down her cheeks, Daisy sank to the ground holding Ben's photo close to her. Tears united them, spoke the same message, overwhelmed them. Groups of pilgrims filled the square. Some sat, some stood, hugged, reached out. Emotions were palpable, all had a story to tell, experiences to share.

'We've done it, we've bloody done it.'

The end of a momentous journey so meaningful for each summed up by Bryony in a few words as the friends hugged each other. She winced but said nothing as Daisy hung onto her arm. They stood, silent and awestruck at the towering spires rising to a now clearing sky, a monument to St James and all those who followed in his footsteps, and as if on cue the clouds parted to salute their success.

'Can I make a suggestion?' Bryony finally broke the silence. 'It's well past midday, we've missed today's service. Let's have a drink, we should toast our success, stop for a minute, absorb what we've achieved. Then you need to offload your backpack. The cathedral will be here tomorrow. Am I being selfish? Can you wait until then? Be honest.'

By way of an answer, Daisy removed the weight from her shoulders.

'Let me just sit awhile, take it all in. Then one drink, a shower and change. I do need to eat, I'm starving, then we can get our bearings. We're here, what if Ben's here? I've got to start making enquiries. But I agree, cathedral tomorrow.'

The two friends found a nearby bar and sat in companionable silence, each with a cider, each with their own thoughts. Bryony then led Daisy to their accommodation where she unpacked, showered and dressed in more comfortable clothes. Both tied their shells to their day bags; an acknowledgement of their pilgrim status, and put their phones in their pockets, each had their own reason, neither questioned the other.

It didn't take long to choose a restaurant with outdoor seating in the back garden. Vines twisted through the weathered timber supports giving protection from the sun, so necessary at the height of the summer, but pleasant as decoration on this occasion.

A bottle of red wine with olives and bread arrived.

'Cheers, salud, well done to my wonderful friend, we've made it.' Bryony smiled broadly as she raised her glass, Daisy returned the sentiment.

'Thank you, dear Bryony, and I do mean 'dear Bryony'. I would never have made it without you by my side when I needed you most.'

'Bloody hell, Daisy, we're getting all sentimental now, we're going to end up tearful again.'

'It's true,' came the simple reply.

As they ate, they shared their respective stories. Daisy was bursting with emotion as she related her meeting with Camille and Mateus at Casa Bonita. She then hesitantly explained Nicolas's thoughts on Ben possibly suffering from amnesia, which to her relief Bryony agreed was a credible reason for his disappearance.

'We can't rule anything out until we have proof otherwise.'

Daisy smiled at the 'We'.

Bryony again touched upon her overnight stay at the Casa

195

Rural and her time with Miguel but did elaborate on her accident and time with Jack.

'Did either of us have any idea how the Camino was going to have such an impact when we set off?'

'Isn't that why we're here?' came Daisy's philosophical answer, posed as a question.

They discussed what to do for the rest of the evening as the wine flowed.

'Now we're here I don't actually know where to start. Should we go round handing out leaflets, I need a photocopy shop, I wonder where Patrick is?' Daisy gabbled on as if their arrival had temporarily triggered a loss of direction within her.

Bryony stepped in and offered her thoughts, which is how they found themselves strolling the alleys in the half light of the evening. They acquainted themselves with the now closed Pilgrims Office and a hostel worth visiting the following day for potential Ben information. They then headed for the evening tranquility of a park which looked out over towards the cathedral.

Part 3, Leon to Santiago

13

Three meet in Santiago and Onwards...

'ANY IDEA WHERE this bar is? It can't be far away, can it? D'you remember seeing it when you were with Jack?' Daisy fumbled in her bag trying to locate her phone.

Bryony took hers from her pocket and passed it over. 'I can't even remember what Patrick said it was called.'

'Cafe Bar ... something ... I think.' Daisy located the map of Santiago on Bryony's phone and widened the screen. 'Yes, here it is. Cafe Bar Pedro, turn left, second right and it's near the Pilgrim Office. We must go there afterwards to collect our Compostelas. Are you ready? I don't want to be late.'

The two girls had returned to their hotel the previous evening marvelling at having seen Patrick in the park so soon after arriving in Santiago. They had agreed to meet up with him for breakfast at nine thirty and now Daisy was pacing the corridor outside their rooms, her room key jangling in her hand.

Bryony locked her door, then adjusted her sling with one hand and hugged her friend with the other.

'Too right I'm ready. Blood, sweat and tears, both of us. I need the certificate as proof for the girls back home, and you -for your friends and your mum and dad ... and maybe Ben. Your quest is not over yet, girl. Right, onwards and upwards to meet Patrick.'

Santiago was already buzzing as pilgrims, locals and tourists wandered, languages of the world mixed and swirled as a

199

universal sense of joy pervaded. The lanes and alleys were beginning to warm as the sun strengthened.

Two cappuccinos were ordered and the girls sat in companionable silence.

'Are we in the right place?' Daisy looked at her watch. 'We've been here half an hour now. How reliable is he? He was a bit strange last night. I want to get going.' She picked up her bag.

'Buenos dias, señoras.' The third chair at the table was suddenly scraped back as Patrick sat down. He immediately stood up, kissed each girl on the cheek, called for a cafe negro and returned to his seat.

'Did you get to the pilgrim service yesterday?' He directed the first question and Bryony explained their plan, in reply he suggested they order breakfast, explaining they should aim to be at the cathedral by 11.30 to get a seat.

'Before we go any further ... Daisy, I need to make one phone call which I'll do when you're at the service and I may, I said may be able to give you some information about Ben. Please don't get your hopes up too much, this is a very tenuous link. I thought I'd tell you now before you start probing me. All I can say, there is a guy, not here in Santiago at the moment, who may know something. I've never met him, all I know is he's due back today from ... somewhere, seeing his folks or something. So, please be patient, all I've got is a phone number, nothing else.'

Daisy cupped her mouth as if to stifle a response, Bryony reached out to her whilst Patrick tactfully veered the conversation towards a more superficial topic. Daisy composed herself as they shared their stories following their meeting in Burgos, possibly some details were omitted, maybe some were exaggerated. Patrick and Bryony chatted amicably; Daisy quietly listened on.

Beneath the camaraderie however, lay the direction of each of their futures. Three pilgrims from different backgrounds who individually set out weeks ago, with the desire to have questions answered, to be able to move on in their respective lives. Their physical journeys had been achieved, their personal needs now required a conclusion, for two of them their destiny was in their respective hands, for Daisy, it was still the unknown. Names emerged, Ben, Jack, Miguel, Ma, Gran – names of people to maybe help shape their individual futures. Three emotional, frank and engaging stories.

They eventually agreed to meet again in the late afternoon. Patrick and Bryony shared an unobtrusive glance towards each other and at Daisy, who had gone very quiet. Bryony nodded to him as if she had read his mind and with that he was gone.

The two girls made for the cathedral in time to find seats towards the front of the nave. As with each daily service, pilgrims and tourists from around the world gathered, united in the bond to participate in one of the most moving daily acts of worship. Voices became hushed as the priests and choir took their seats and the sonorous incantation began. Bryony moved closer to Daisy as she felt her hand being sought. The understanding did not matter; it was the spiritual sense of belonging.

The congregation vied for a better view to greet the start of the spectacle; eight men in red robes positioning themselves at the front of the cathedral preparing to swing the mighty incense burner. Smoke filled the interior as the men swung the ropes holding the burner; a strong, sweet smell of incense pervaded, historically burned to cloud the smell of unwashed, dirty pilgrims. Daisy became inconsolable, Bryony did her best to offer support in a discreet way and as the service came to its conclusion, they returned to the sunlight of the plaza. Bryony brushed off Daisy's apology, encouraging her to engage in the wonder of the spectacle they had experienced and the feeling of peace which seemed to emanate. She then put her good arm around her friend's shoulder.

'Look Daisy, this is your day. I'm here to help you with anything you want to do. We've plenty of time before we meet Patrick. Shall we get our Compostelas first or go to the hostel? Your choice.'

The short queue at the Pilgrims Office made their decision easy and within half an hour the two girls came out into the sunlight clutching their certificates, each suitably rolled into a cardboard tube.

'Congratulations dear friend, so well deserved.'

'You and me both,' answered Daisy.

'Latin was never my strong point but I can just about recognise my name.'

Daisy smiled back at Bryony's light-hearted comment as she too studied her beautifully inscribed certificate.

They made their way to the hostel which luckily for them was being reopened after lunch. Following introductions, Daisy explained her mission as she showed the photo of Ben. The manager's English was not good but they made themselves understood with basic words and signs.

'Looks familiar but, not sure, many pilgrims stay.' He pointed to the surroundings. 'You say two years ago? Yesterday, Pedro from other hostel he asked me about a missing English person, said he had been asked by another pilgrim.'

Daisy got the gist of what he was saying.

'Patrick!' the two girls spoke in unison.

Daisy fidgeted as they thanked the manager, she grabbed Bryony's good arm and pulled her out into the alleyway. It was nearly time to meet up with Patrick so there was only one place to head for. They shared a plate of tapas and a half flagon of cider. Daisy looked regularly at her watch and walked around the plaza as if willing Patrick to appear. Bryony sat and enjoyed the sunshine.

'Kathleen!' a shout came from across the square. People watched as Daisy ran towards Patrick.

'Well, did you make the phone call?'

He had ... Jonno was back in Santiago, Patrick had contacted him, there was a possibility he could help but they would need to meet him at his place of work, just outside Santiago on the road to Finisterre.

'Taxi, I'll pay, can we go now? Will you come with us?'

Daisy returned to the table. 'Oh my God, thank you, thank you, are you coming Bryony?' She picked up her day bag.

'Where can we get a taxi?'

Patrick and Bryony exchanged nods and smiles as he took charge. Twenty minutes later the taxi drove up an unmade lane and stopped at a bar with an outside seating area. It looked out over a small field with overripe grape vines on one side and another stony unattended field on the other. The bar itself appeared in need of attention; a slightly ragged blind over the front of it gave shelter from the sun and the few wooden chairs and tables scattered around had seen better days. A young man was serving drinks to a couple of elderly men.

'Jonno?' Patrick called out. The young man looked in their direction.

'Are you Jonno?' Daisy repeated as she took Ben's photo from her bag and made towards him.

'Make or break time,' Bryony muttered under her breath.

'Yes, that's me. Why? Can I get you a drink?' He offered them a table.

Patrick suggested to Daisy he start the conversation.

'I'm not being rude or anything but ...' he hesitated, 'I'm involved but unbiased. Perhaps I could start the story factually, without emotions taking over? I'm a little worried he might not know anything about Ben and then you'll be ...' he allowed the sentence to fade. 'You can step in, take over, however you want to play it and I'll bow out.'

Daisy half nodded and passed Ben's picture to Patrick. He in turn showed it to Jonno.

'What I'm about to give you is a potted version of Daisy's quest. This is Ben, Daisy's son, he disappeared after passing through Burgos two years ago. She's been on a search for him. Ben sent her a postcard from Burgos, since then – nothing. Spanish police have drawn a blank too. Coincidentally I met him when I was doing the walk – this is my second time – and more coincidentally, Daisy and I met a few weeks ago, she showed me his photo as we both sat eating lunch outside a bar. Whether he actually completed the Camino she doesn't know. Some other people she met knew of him, the girl especially. It was suggested he might be suffering from some sort of amnesia; I don't know why. Pedro, at the hostel where I'm staying here in Santiago, said he knew of you and your English contacts, you were worth trying, so here we are.'

He looked towards Daisy as if to seek affirmation and handed her back the photo.

'This is Ben, my Ben.'

Jonno took the somewhat dog-eared photo from her. 'I'm so sorry, that's some story. You must be desperate to know what's happened.' He halted then looked across at her. 'You say this is your son?'

'Yes, Ben.' She looked enquiringly at him.

'This sort of looks like a guy I know – knew – guy called Shaun, looks neat and tidy here. If it is him, he's scruffier with dreadlocks now. Well, was the last time I saw him.'

'Shaun, that's Ben's dad's name,' Daisy whispered.

There was an intake of breath from Bryony.

Patrick took the photo and stared at Ben's face. 'A man of differing personalities. Sorry Daisy, I wasn't insulting him, it's just, oh I don't know, don't know what to say.'

'What don't you know?' asked Jonno.

'Oh nothing, just me with my big mouth, forget it.'

'When did you last see Be– Shaun?'

'Sit down, I'll get us all a drink and tell you what I can.'

Jonno left the table and returned with a bottle of brandy and four glasses. He passed a glass to each, Patrick downed his in one, Bryony followed, Daisy sipped and pulled a face.

'Not your favourite drink I guess?' Jonno's smile relieved the tension.

'Where is he now? Tell me what you know.' The one question she didn't ask remained in the air.

It wasn't a long story but it did seem to confirm Shaun could indeed be Ben. For the second time on her journey, it was a Ben not instantly recognisable to Daisy.

Jonno explained how Shaun, as he called him, had been helping with bar work. Had turned up one day last year, with a scruffy, dark blue backpack.

'That's what he left home with.'

'He asked if I had a room in exchange for work. That's how he ended up staying here. He seemed to live in the same clothes until I gave him work clothes. A bit introvert. He didn't offer up much about himself but was a good worker.'

Jonno got the impression Shaun had worked in a bar before as he seemed to know what to do. They didn't socialise much despite him offering on occasions to take Shaun when he went out. He seemed to walk a lot when he wasn't on duty and Jonno sensed he was a bit depressed, a bit of a loner, (as he called him), never seemed relaxed, easily lost in his own thoughts. They chatted but didn't confide, however he did recall an occasion when out of the blue Shaun mentioned boarding schools not being all they're cracked up to be. Church on Sunday and a lot of bullying. At the time Jonno couldn't understand why Shaun suddenly confided this to him and the subject was dropped. The topic of families did not arise and Jonno hadn't thought it his place to delve. Then on another random occasion he referred to a past girlfriend but didn't elaborate.

'Camille?' Daisy turned to Patrick who shrugged his shoulders, nodding his head at the same time.

'Did he drink? Smoke?' Patrick posed the question which surprised Daisy as she had never known Ben to do either.

'Drink? Yeh. Smoke? Well, we shared a joint on occasions, if that's what you mean. Mine, not his, but I got the impression it wasn't his first time.'

'Depressed and we didn't notice. Who was bullying him? What were they doing? Why didn't he tell us?' Daisy said to no one in particular.

Bryony put her arm around Daisy's shoulders.

'Maybe he didn't want to worry you. Maybe all this time later and without realising, he sensed trust in Jonno. Needed to tell someone.'

Then one morning after a rare few drinks the previous evening, Shaun became angry when Jonno said he was going to have to let him go, there wasn't enough work to keep him on. He put Shaun in touch with a mate who ran a bar and was rebuilding disused accommodation with a view to turning it into a hostel for pilgrims. It was nearer to Finisterre and he believed Ben might still be there.

He was. Following a phone call to the bar, it was decided Jonno would drive Daisy who by now was so on edge she agreed to the decisions without question. The other two agreed to stay behind and offered to look after the place, Patrick insisting that he too had done bar work back in Ireland. He didn't elaborate on which side of the bar he meant.

✦

'Did he have a birthmark on his stomach?' were the only words spoken by Daisy during the short journey.

'Do I look the sort to know what another man has on his stomach?' Jonno laughed, as he kept the answer light, choosing instead to point out various places along the way.

He finally drew up in front of a bar recently renovated, wooden benches with umbrellas advertising a well-known cider were dotted around. Tubs filled with geraniums and cacti gave colour under the cloudless sky. A fig tree emerged from a dusty, neglected patch to one side of the bar where a half-finished restoration project stood. The sound of a drill could be heard.

Jonno put his arm around Daisy's shoulder and guided her towards the door.

'No turning back now.'

An empty bar greeted them. Jonno walked up to the counter where a selection of cakes and baguettes were on display. He introduced himself and showed Ben's photo to a girl washing glasses. He spoke fluent Spanish to her and she nodded in return. Daisy hesitated in the doorway.

'Si.' A simple word that spoke volumes.

'Let's wait outside, Shaun is here, he's working across the yard.' Jonno carried a tray with three glasses as he led Daisy to a bench.

The girl emerged from the barn with a young man sporting reddish coloured dreadlocks and wearing shorts and a T-shirt, both of which had seen better days. Daisy rushed to him photo in hand.

'Ben, Ben. Oh my God, it is you!' She flung herself at him, he stiffened and looked over her head towards Jonno.

'Jonno, mate, what are you doing here? What the hell…?'

'Shaun, come and sit down.'

Shaun responded to the name and politely backed away from Daisy who blinked back tears as she followed. She put the photo on the table and allowed Jonno to speak, then pushed the photo towards Ben who tentatively picked it up, staring hard at the face staring back at him. Her eyes never wavered from Ben, his hands, his long fingers – her father's fingers.

'I'm sorry, who's this? Should I know him?'

He didn't recognise himself.

'Ben – Shaun – I'm Daisy, your mum. This photo was taken just before you set off on the Camino. To raise funds for Sam's charity. Remember Sam? And Mike? Your friends in Ipswich? Mike was going to come with you? Do you remember them?'

Daisy's voice became higher pitched, Jonno gently placed his hand on her arm.

Ben continued to look at the photo, a slight frown on his face. Daisy went to touch his hand, for just a second she made contact, squeezed before he withdrew it to lift his glass.

'Beautiful fingers, just like your grandfather's. D'you remember your grandfather? He made you a stick to bring with you, with a carved head.'

Shaun looked puzzled. Daisy glanced at Jonno who mouthed a word, 'Patience.'

Silence followed as he stood up.

'So buddy, Shaun, how you getting on here? How's the building work going?'

Jonno certainly knew when to diffuse tension; Shaun looked across to the barn, Daisy relaxed her tensed shoulders.

'It's good. D'you want to see it?'

'Sure.'

The two young men made their way across the yard, Daisy

chose not to follow. She sat for a while allowing the warmth of the sun to permeate her mind and wash over her muddled thoughts. A couple of pilgrims arrived; she offered a 'Bon Camino' to which they reciprocated with a cheery 'Ola.' She looked at her watch and eventually made her way over to the barn and stood where the doorway would eventually be. Ben and Jonno were deep in conversation and did not see her arrive.

'Your mum ... searching ... son ...'

She watched Ben; a look of confusion on his face. He sat on the earth floor and put his head in his hands. Jonno brushed his fingers through his hair, a frown clouding his face. This was too much for Daisy who rushed in and sat alongside Ben, Jonno quietly left them alone.

Daisy eventually emerged into the softness of the early evening. She was alone but a lightness of emotion accompanied her. She nodded at Jonno, mouthing three words.

'It is him.' Her face said it all as she touched her tummy. 'Birthmark.'

She walked past the cafe towards a neglected field where dusty wild cactus grew lopsidedly out from the dry earth. Jonno watched as she receded into the distance, he ordered three soft drinks and waited. The sound of drilling returned, he looked towards Daisy, now a faint dot on the evening landscape, then towards the barn. He took two of the glasses and offered one to Shaun and went and sat outside. Shaun eventually followed.

Two young men sitting, sharing a drink, talk punctuated by silences, an easy friendship to any passer-by.

It was a while later and almost dark when Daisy reappeared, she didn't say anything, neither did Ben. Jonno looked at his watch, made eye contact with her and moved towards his car.

'Shall I see you tomorrow?'

As she spoke Daisy reached across to Ben, he tentatively allowed her to take his hand, then withdrew it as he gave a shrug and a nod in reply. He stood and watched as Jonno turned the car round. Daisy turned to wave, but he had already made his way back into the barn.

'It is him, isn't it? The birthmark, his long fingers.'

Daisy broke the silence as they headed back to Patrick and Bryony. No questions were needed, Daisy's face said it all. Hugs with words back and forth tripping over each other, unfinished sentences, more excitable hugs ... a journey fulfilled.

Daisy started telling the story then paused and looked at her watch.

'Give me ten minutes, I must phone Shaun, and Mum and Dad.'

As they waited, Patrick helped Jonno clear empty glasses from the tables and when she returned it was Patrick who declared that despite wanting to hear all the good news, they needed to think about returning to Santiago.

Part 4, Events Unfold

14

Meeting Shaun, Meeting Ben

I T WAS LATE when we finally returned to our hotel in Santiago. Patrick had phoned his hostel and Pedro agreed to wait up for him, and as a courtesy Bryony had contacted our hotel. We opened a bottle of wine and sat on my bed talking well into the night. I showed her the photo of Ben on my phone hardly daring to believe it was him. She was wonderful, she listened, she comforted me, she said all the right things as I recounted detail after detail.

She held my hand as I explained how on the phone back at the bar, Shaun had broken down; how he and I had cried together as I explained where I was, where I had been and how we had found Ben – thanks to Patrick's doggedness and the birthmark. She kept my glass topped up as I explained how he reacted when I told him Ben was calling himself Shaun and how he admitted to feelings of deep guilt over the past few weeks knowing I was out here searching whilst he was back home. What I didn't admit to her was how I felt a little let down by him not joining me at any stage of my journey. After all Ben was his son as much as mine. OK, I had said not to come out but a little bit of me had hoped he might ignore that and join in my search even if only for a short while. Bryony laughed when I explained he was now all for coming out to join me as Dad and Sam had offered to do earlier in the walk.

'Men are like buses: nothing, then three come along together.'

I smiled as her humour diffused the intensity building up in the room. She suggested it wouldn't be a good idea for anyone to join me at this point – for Ben's sake. I agreed, at the same time admitting I just wanted him all to myself for a while.

As we talked, I could hear my words tripping over each other and at one point Bryony brought me down to earth by gently reminding me the days ahead could be difficult. Hers became the voice of reason reminding me Ben may be reluctant to engage more or worse still, suddenly deny everything and disappear. Our conversation stalled as I tried to put myself in his shoes, see this from his point of view, but I couldn't. I wasn't the one with amnesia ... or, is he even suffering from it? If he is, why? What is going on in his mind? What has been the trigger? So many questions but no answers until expert advice has been sought and that has not even been broached. Then there was the presence of Mateus and Camille which will eventually need to be disclosed and thinking about them reminded me I needed to contact Camille, a job to be done first thing in the morning. So much to contemplate, no wonder my brain hurt.

Bryony yawned and lay down on my bed. Two am and my thoughts were still in overdrive as she snored! Rather than disturb her I slipped into her room.

As I lay there another problem surfaced; if he is prepared to acknowledge he is Ben, the boy in the photo, will he then agree to return to the UK? I knew nothing about this brain disorder but knew enough to recognise he needed professional help and be willing to accept it. Might it be a good idea to suggest Shaun does join us? Might it help if Ben recognised his dad? So much hinged on his state of mind. A jumble of questions with no answers and this was only the beginning or – God forbid – what happens if it is the end? What happens if tomorrow he insists that he is Shaun, denies everything, refuses to engage?

No wonder I hardly slept.

The sun streamed through the window the following morning as I sat on the side of the bed talking on the phone to Camille. The excitement in her voice said it all and this time it was me being the voice of reason as I reminded her we were far from getting Ben back, in more ways than one. I promised I would phone again following today's meeting with him. I put the phone down on an extremely excited young lady hoping that, like me, she did not raise her hopes too far.

By 9.00am Patrick was outside our hotel with a taxi. I had agreed to meet Jonno at nine thirty and he alone would take me to meet up with Ben. Patrick wanted to be with us but was happy to go along with any decisions made. Bryony decided to stay behind.

'I'd be in the way and I've got things to do.'

Wrapped in my own emotions I didn't even pursue her cryptic statement.

The cafe was closed and we had to bang on the door twice to raise Jonno. A sombre face greeted us.

'I've just come off the phone. Maria, the girl who works there, said Ben's bed hasn't been slept in.'

'Shit, man.' Patrick's two words said it all. He told me later that I shouted, 'No' he can't!' and he thought I was having a heart attack. I don't remember anything until I was given a paper bag to blow in and a glass of brandy thrust into my hands. Jonno and Patrick decided after all, the three of us should make for the bar, speak to Maria and 'take it from there.' I was too stressed to argue.

Maria allowed me into Ben's room or 'Shaun's room' as she called it. The dark navy rucksack, now well-worn was leaning against the wall. I touched it but refrained from delving. I didn't recognise any of the clothing but realised two years on it's not surprising. His passport came to mind; no passport meant not being able to leave the country which calmed me a little, and much as I wanted to check through the cupboards and drawers, I knew it was not my place to do so just in case he walked in on me or, worse still, it wasn't Ben, even though the birthmark proved otherwise.

The walking stick carved by his granddad was nowhere to be seen but that didn't surprise or disappoint me. Patrick has never mentioned that Ben used one and sticks are frequently

213

left by their owners, including me, outside bars, hostels or cafes. Idly I wondered who might be the current 'owners' of both his walking stick and mine and hoped whoever they were, their journeys were being made a little easier. I was saddened to acknowledge this could be any young man's room but was heartened to believe he can't have disappeared for ever otherwise he would have taken his possessions. He intended returning but when? And for how long do I wait?

Fleetingly I felt sick to think I might be returning to the UK without Ben. I had raised the hopes of Shaun and Mum and Dad, not to mention my own. Irrationally, I also felt cross with him for putting us through this. Was he even aware of how his actions might have such repercussions on others? I knew nothing about what was going on in his head. Physically he was Ben, mentally he was Shaun. How on earth could the two be reconciled? I returned downstairs to join Jonno and Patrick sitting at a table outside. An uncomfortable silence lodged between the three of us, there wasn't much we could say, it had all been said.

I looked across the field I had sought solace in the previous day. My eyes suddenly fixed on a dot in the distance which appeared to be slowly increasing in size. Jonno and Patrick chatted as I strained my head towards the outline of a moving person. It was him, Ben, looking dishevelled, walking wearily in our direction. My heart encouraged me to run to him, my brain put the brakes on.

'Jonno, Daisy. Sorry I wasn't here when you arrived.'

That was all he said. He looked towards Patrick, frowning but unquestioning.

Patrick went to stand up.

'Ben?'

There was no response, or was there? Did I detect a hint of recognition?

Jonno then complicated things by addressing him as Shaun as he introduced Patrick, who, to his credit kept things simple by way of return.

I sensed Maria's inquisitiveness as she brought out four

coffees, I nodded and smiled my thanks. Ben continued standing as I showed him his photo again and this time added the somewhat creased postcard he had sent from Burgos. All he commented on was the size of the cathedral, no mention of being with anyone, no mention of any incidences, nothing to help us fill in any gaps. I glanced at Patrick who seemed to be willing Ben to say more, without success. It was frustrating but we had to accept we needed to tread lightly and slowly.

I explained what Patrick had told me, keeping details simple and sparing. We had agreed I would do the talking this time as didn't want to confuse him with too many people offering too many facts. We were doing this 'on the hoof' as Bryony had earlier suggested, we were hardly experts after all. We had also agreed to introduce the names of his gran and grandad and bring his dad into the conversation. Also mention his two friends, Mike and Sam, but leave Camille and Mateus for now. An overload of information could have an adverse effect on him.

It's amazing the difference a day makes.

He acknowledged yesterday's visit but didn't go as far as accepting what we had disclosed. He did explain his overnight disappearance as, 'Something I do sometimes when I need to think.' That sounded hopeful.

He seemed more acceptant of our presence but still guarded in his attitude towards us. Let's face it, we were announcing to him the fact he had been living a lie these past months – we had proof of who he, Ben, was, he had no proof he was or wasn't Shaun. That must have been a very unsettling situation to be confronted with. He mentioned he had no passport, said he had lost it and never got round to replacing or finding out how to.

We kept to superficial facts we could confirm, from the birthmark to Patrick suddenly announcing Ben had a scar on his upper left leg, the result of falling over a stone wall. There was such a scar. I gasped. Ben went quiet as if trying to process this revelation. Amongst all the questions I wanted to ask there was one that Bryony had said I should not put to him, but I did.

'Ben, Shaun, are you happy?'

Then another.

'Do you, do you ever think about – want to know about – your past?'

Patrick laid an arm on mine. I sensed I had gone too far.

Ben did not answer immediately.

'Past? I'm not sure – sometimes. I don't know.'

I had to be content with that even though it broke my heart to accept this was my son answering. He began to shuffle from one foot to another and look towards the barn, it was as if he was needing the security of something familiar to him, to be in control of his surroundings.

There was no more to say, no more I could do and amidst all this emotion I knew I had to face my return to the UK, I couldn't put it off any longer. Mum, Dad, Shaun, my girl-friends from the village – I couldn't wait to share Ben with them but I also needed to get back to work. My boss had been wonderful but I had certainly stretched his tolerance where an extension to my unpaid leave had been concerned. It would be a bittersweet end to my journey but it had to be faced.

Our goodbyes were restrained, despite my being desperate to hug and hang onto Ben. Patrick laid his hand on Ben's arm and suddenly announced in a nonchalant way his decision to stay on in Spain for a while and help out in Jonno's bar. A hint of a glance in my direction spoke volumes.

Beyond my wildest dreams I had accomplished all I set out to do, I knew I had to accept he may reject returning to the UK but at the same time practicalities for his possible return had to be addressed and I hadn't a clue where to start. Shaun and Dad were going to have to take over and their earlier respective offers to come here might even be realised and necessary. On a frivolous point and completely irrelevant Bryony had also commented last night that the first thing I needed to do on my return was get a good haircut and facial.

'With those wild red tresses and sunburned face anyone would think you've been working in the fields.'

A humorous point and honest to the end but such a suggestion was the last thing on my mind even if it was true.

15

Decision time

Bryony

I<small>T IS IMPORTANT</small> that Daisy should return to Ben unencumbered by me. Take Patrick, fine he knows Ben, even if Ben appears not to recognise him. Daisy needs moral support and Patrick is the one to be by her side.

I have things to do anyway, final decisions to make that I can't put off much longer. Booking my flight back to the UK is number one task. I have so many mixed feelings about my future and in fairness to Jack, returning home is priority, even if it's not to be for ever. Alongside my completed physical journey lies the decision regarding my continued personal journey – through my future life as Bryony not just as Mrs Davidson – or even maybe reverting to my maiden name- if that is to be.

I have achieved one of the most momentous experiences in my life, physically, mentally and emotionally. Being here in Santiago has given me time to reflect on the highs and lows of the past weeks. This adventure has tested me to my limits but I've loved every minute of it even if at times I've sworn to the heavens and given in to the devil on my shoulder. Blisters, sprained ankle, broken collar bone, in all the years I've lived as a suburban housewife – God, how I hate that expression – I have never experienced even one of those injuries.

The weigh scales of this adventure have been weighted heavily on the side of the angel who guided me, protected me, walked with me. I've been allowed to listen to the devil, permit it to intrude on the odd occasion (for my own sanity of course) but then the scales have tipped back and I've been reined in again. Could I contemplate returning to my old life of coffee dates, shopping and girls' days out? When I think about it, I now realise all these did was mask the deteriorating relationship between Jack and me. We've carried out a respectable job of putting on a front with friends and family, we're still good mates but it is now time for complete honesty. We said a lot to each other last week but we reined in at final decisions. He's a good man, we've both got time ahead of us and I need greater fulfilment in my life however that may unfold, and I reckon he does too.

He said I'd changed, looked more natural, acted differently. I took that as a compliment; it's true, this walk has had such an impact on me, I feel different, this is the new me.

As I internalised all these thoughts, I looked at myself in the full-length mirror in the bedroom. I liked who I saw staring back. The slightly unruly hair suits me, the excess around my middle has lessened. My skin is tanned, my eyes are bright. Even flat walking shoes, T-shirt and creased trousers are in keeping and suit my figure. I'm smiling, I sensed I do a fair amount of that these days. I am still Bryony but the new Bryony.

Jack had hinted at 'other female company' having 'turned his head.' He said he would always love me; did that mean he was not in love with me? Indeed, was I in love with him? Were I to return and pick up from where we had left off, would our life merely jog along, each living a lie? Wasting valuable time when we could be exploring other options – whatever they may be. What happens if we stay together and then it's too late to move on? Could I move out and live alone? Do I want a solitary life? Apartment or house? Pet or no pet? My mind was racing.

I'm looking forward to seeing the girls. All their light-hearted albeit sceptical comments seem a lifetime ago. I looked again at myself in the mirror and imagined turning up for a coffee date wearing a T-shirt, walking sandals and cotton trousers. I would have the last laugh.

Thoughts flood my mind, rational and irrational. Thoughts for which I have no definitive answers.

Daisy worries me still. What is she going to do? What would I do if I were in her shoes? I've loved her company, I admire her tenacity, she's done this walk with one thought in mind. I'm not convinced I would have stuck at it; maybe that's what being a mum is all about, practically giving your life for your child. We'll stay in touch at the very least. I need to know how the Ben saga pans out. As for Patrick, bless him. Maybe we'll share the odd text from him, random no doubt. He deserves to find someone, somewhere.

Within half an hour I'd booked my flight and acknowledged a rumbling tummy. It's another warm day, ideal for indulgent actions and to get rid of the last of my euros, so a final wander around Santiago will serve both purposes.

A small dish with a shell painted on it caught my eye, then a pair of canvas espadrilles, yellow of all colours, my favourite although never before on a shoe. Old shopping habits die hard as I succumbed to their presence, the devil and the angel still fluttering. I stopped to listen to a busker and watch a small troupe of dancers in national costume. The atmosphere was joyous, good natured and infectious.

As with the last few days I have spent alone after Jack left, I feel safe and regardless of no decisions made I am at peace with myself. For whatever reason I just love this city and how the atmosphere of the alleys draw me in. Suddenly Daisy appears - and is gone again, I wonder how is she getting on? I do hope she phones before I leave, I could phone her but truth be told I'm a bit anxious in case things have gone pear-shaped. Maybe, if there's time at the airport, I will.

As I browse, a menu on a blackboard outside a restaurant draws my eye. Its name highlighted in large print at the top of the board – Miguel's. No, it can't be him, he didn't mention anything about a business in Santiago. Memories of my brief stop at his hotel, the beautiful garden, the view across to the Meseta, his gentle company, his heartache, undiminished by time – fill my mind. Had I read too much into the way he folded a stray piece of hair back behind my ear as we bade our farewells? I took a seat at a table for two by the window. Chicken paella is on offer. The last time I had enjoyed that meal was back with him in Hornillos. My hand itches with the desire to dig out my phone, I resist.

'Don't complicate matters.' I suddenly realise I'm talking aloud as I wait for the meal to arrive. It may be a coincidence, Miguel is a typically Spanish name, but it doesn't mean I have to give in to it – not at this moment anyway.

My last meal, my last day in Santiago, my last opportunity to savour the beauty of the city and its cathedral, its history, its people. Those who, as pilgrims, like me, arrive exhausted but triumphant, passing through the gates with their own stories to tell and successes to savour.

'I want more of this. This is me.'

Without thinking, I take my phone from my day bag and scroll down until Miguel's number appears, safely tucked in between that of my friend Maggie and my hairdresser Moll. I stop myself again.

Not now – later maybe.

Definitely.

Daisy

I walked the Camino to find my son, I found my son because I walked the Camino. Every time I think that I start grinning – ear to ear as they say. I want to shout it to the world.

'I HAVE FOUND MY SON!'

Mum and Dad can't believe it, Shaun initially wanted to come out, the girls have texted me with delight and can't wait for the champagne evening. Bryony kept hugging me, Patrick's being wonderful with keeping an eye on Ben and I'm on top of the world. It almost hurts when I start thinking about it all. There he is, not a million miles away, I've touched him, looked into his eyes, steadied my heart more times than I care to think about.

It's so difficult to accept this is my last evening in Spain, final meal in Santiago. Shame I'll be eating alone but I can indulge myself, eat where I want and when I want. Sit and gaze into the future – with Ben, please God. Last time I'll be heaving my backpack into position, suffering minor panics in case I don't reach my nightly destination along the way. Remembering to buy enough water to get me through. How lovely it'll be to only have to fill a bottle from the kitchen tap.

I can't believe how hard it was to say goodbye to Bryony. I had left the hotel in the morning never thinking that she might be gone by the time I returned from Finisterre. We spoke on the phone as Patrick and I returned to Santiago. She was on her way to the airport. Promises to keep in touch were shared, and I cried (yet again) when she told me she had a 'farewell gift' for me – she had paid the bill on the hotel including tonight.

It seems an age since I left the security of my village. Flying from Stansted and arriving at St Jean Pied de Port alone and terrified is still vividly imprinted on my mind. I've never done anything like this before.

The days, weeks and months following Ben's disappearance

were spent living near to my parents with friends always close at hand in the village. I'd been rarely alone unless I chose to be and to be honest that had not been often. Since Ben's disappearance I've always minimised time by myself, reckoning that being surrounded by others diminishes negative thoughts. Gosh, this has been some undertaking and a massive leap into the unknown but I have found him.

When I think about it, my first few Camino days must have passed in a flurry of anxiety and fear for my physical and mental well-being, not to mention being exhausted on reaching each overnight stay. Was I capable? Would I make it? Would I give in? What if blisters were so painful I couldn't walk properly? What if I got lost? Well, none of those happened, apart from the odd blister and … oh … and finding my son. The hostels were fine for youngsters but were a bit of an endurance. I think I can allow myself a feeling of smugness that I used them more than Bryony but am not surprised; she really isn't cut out for basic living. Give her credit though she made it to the end, with a little bit – well actually quite a big bit – of help along the way!

I've surprised myself with my strength of character and determination to keep going. I like to think it has been Ben's spirit alongside me, driving me ever closer to his physical presence. Whatever it was, it worked and I have the photo to prove it.

The journey has had its highs and lows, but I guess that applies to everyone who treads its path. Everyone sets out as a pilgrim for their own reasons; Bryony and Patrick are prime examples. I guess everyone who reaches Santiago will have achieved their personal goal but, when I think about it, most do not continue onwards to the end of the world at Finisterre. Without planning to, the three of us nearly did – all thanks to Ben. Maybe, if all goes well and in time, we – Mum, Dad, Ben and me – could return to complete that part of the route. If … so many ifs, let's not get carried away, one thing at a time.

If though, I did have to choose one part that stands out, what would it be? Santo Domingo? Finding the lucky white feather, still tucked in my backpack. Gorgeous parador, apart from the cathedral bells ringing every fifteen minutes. Burgos? Meeting dear Bryony and Patrick for the first time, well, second time for Patrick, thank you Patrick for what you're doing now. I hope Ben and you are getting on OK. That was a lovely time sitting in the shadow of the cathedral, sharing confidences. That city was where my journey really began. O'Cebreiro? God, that was difficult, awful, but I climbed it, marvelled at the pallozas and came out the other side and continued on through mist, fog and chill. Surely though, Casa Bonita? Adorable Mateus and Camille, such a tranquil place. Holding my baby grandchild, sitting with my 'sort of daughter-in-law'. How can I forget? And surely, they'll be with us for life regardless of whatever happens next. Meeting the lovely lady Sophia was brief but of such significance, without realising, she guided me to Bonita and on to where I am now, hers was a voice of reason. In time I will phone her, thank her, explain all to her.

How difficult it has been not to mention their names to Ben. I wonder how he would have reacted? But as Patrick said, it was a risk not worth taking and regardless of how hard it was I know we did the right thing. He needs the services of an expert back home to sort all this out. Why did he choose to disappear? Something must have triggered it. Might there be more to the Camille and Patrick's relationship? What did he mean when he mentioned boarding school to Jonno? I can't bear the thought that something might have happened to him, something I didn't know about. Might he be harbouring guilt over his good health following Sam's death and Mike's illness? Did our divorce affect him more than we realised? Where do we start? Please, please, let him agree to return home, meet everyone, get help, get sorted.

If there's one thing I do regret about this journey, it has been my somewhat lax attitude towards diary keeping. I excuse myself by saying I had so much going on but in reality, I was just neglectful. It's not too late to rectify as memories are crystal clear and with them I have the added impetus of creating 'my story' for Ben. I will do it.

I set out on this journey as Daisy, single mum to a missing

child. I'm now back to being a mum, a mother-in-law of sorts and a granny. I'm almost too scared to think about them and how Ben might react when confronted with their existence.

Suffice to say, as a pilgrim, I conquered the Camino and from here I can conquer the next phase of my journey – please God, let it be with Ben.

Patrick

Bloody hell, still in Santiago, still in Spain. Journey's end but stranded. Well, not really stranded, I suppose I did offer to babysit Ben when Daisy said she had to return to the UK. Her face showed it all when the taxi arrived ... wanting, needing, to get home but devastated at the thought of leaving Ben.

I know she's chuffed that I offered and I genuinely meant it but it has left me a bit on my tod. Still, no other great plans around the corner apart from Mum and Gran so another few days won't make any difference. Gran sounds as if she could go on forever and Mum, well, I guess she's OK, seems like her memory's a bit hazy but she sounded with it enough so I'll take my chances. It wasn't as if I'd already promised them anything.

Jonno's told me to make myself at home here, tempting indeed but I have found myself limiting my alcohol intake in favour of lemonade and lime. This is the new me, with responsibility comes moderation and all that.

If you'd told me when I set out all those weeks ago that my first Camino experience would rear up to bite me on the bum I would've laughed in your face. I wasn't even thinking about it, well, not exactly. I guess Dad is still knocking on the door of my past but like last time he's faded into the background as events along the way have overtaken. He's still somewhere, obviously, but that's a topic for me and Mum to get sorted. A reason to get back in touch with her, I guess. I really can't move forward properly until questions have been answered and this Ben thing sorted.

God, what a crap life I've had but maybe this is when I now let go of my past and work towards the future. How weird, I didn't find my Dad but became the catalyst for Daisy finding Ben. Bumping into her sitting outside that bar has been a turning point for me, what were the chances of that? One innocent conversation and here we are, weeks later, Daisy's quest fulfilled, me meeting Camille in Leon and then Ben again and little Mateus of course.

'He's not yours, Patrick.'

Those words hit me in the solar plexus but in a way thank God he isn't, that would've seriously complicated things. Maybe in time she and Ben might meet up, it would be great if I'm around when they do. Daisy's been fantastic in her search and please God let Ben become part of her future. Funny how my first Camino partially centred around him and this one has centred around Daisy, and now him.

He was a decent enough guy, a bit random at times. Drink and he were not good mates, that's for sure, which makes sense having listened to Daisy, a bit Jekyll and Hyde. One too many and it was like a personality transplant going on. OK, like me, his life wasn't exactly 'a bed of roses' as Gran used to say, but whose is these days? Trouble is, I don't think he had the strength or the understanding to deal with it. I don't even know whether he realised how things from your past can affect you. He was an arse at times but then again, he was also great company. He was good with Cammy until I screwed it all up, pardon the phrase. Mind you, she could have said 'No'. I guess we were all as bad as each other, not sticking to the ethos of the Camino. I can sort of understand how it went into free-fall, weeks away from home, freedom, forgetting why they – we – were here. I wonder how much he did confide in her?

We've, well Daisy, has still got the subject of Cammy and the babby to reveal to him, I know she's dying to show the photograph but how can you tell someone who doesn't even know who they actually are, that not a million miles away is an ex-partner with their child? Advice, that's what she's gonna have to seek. It's their family problem now not mine, in fact none of this is my problem, except the minor task of guarding Ben without him realising.

It'll be strange not seeing Bryony again, ships that pass in the night, I guess. I never really felt I got to know her, which is not surprising. Seems as if she's about to kiss goodbye to staid sounding Jack, and I reckon that's good for her.

Sooo ... that leaves me to get sorted.

'The world's your oyster,' Father Dickinson's wise words – God rest his soul.

Last night I worked out I did this in six days less than last time and with a clearer head. It also cost two hundred euros less which can't be bad. If I earn a bit with Jonno and save the rest I'll have a positive wallet when I eventually return to Ireland.

I realise now how these past weeks have been the best ever. I feel fit and healthy, I've met and helped some great people. I've spoken to Gran and Mum, my head feels clear for the first time in ages and I sense my future will pronounce itself to me once I hand my present responsibility over to Daisy and her family.

This journey has taught me three things: 1. Drink is not the answer to all ills. 2. I enjoy investigating people's problems and 3. I love Spain so maybe I do have Spanish blood in me. Maybe I could get some bar work back home, go to Uni as a mature student, study some sort of psychology or whatever, help people with their problems, maybe even Mum ... only joking!

Until then, one more task to fulfil: be here for Ben.

Ben

Thank goodness for Maria. She hasn't asked any questions about my visitors but she knows me well enough to pick up on my mood. After they left, all I said was, 'I'm going to the barn.' She nodded and five minutes later was offering me a cup of coffee.

My head hurt, it felt heavy, my heart was racing. Too much to take in.

She called herself Daisy, my mum, said I was her son? That Shaun was my dad? I left the UK ages ago, so she said. Came here to walk the Camino, something about friends back home. That's a question I didn't think about, where is home? This is my home, well, where I live. The guy with her, Patrick, said we'd been mates, we'd first met in Puente le Reina. I don't remember ever being there but ... there's something about him. He said we'd walked bits of the Camino together, said three of us had. Three not two. Said it as if it meant something but didn't say any more. Saw me again in Burgos, outside the cathedral. Strange, Burgos? Daisy showed me that postcard she said I'd sent from there. God, Burgos, what happened there? Why do I think something happened? Or not actually happened, more a mix of then and ... my brain, it's like cotton wool, I can't get through, go back? Back to where? Burgos? Everything seems to go back to there, but also somewhere else. Another cathedral? Sitting, looking up to the decorated vaulted roof. Me, I think, as a kid in school uniform, crying? Why is he, me? sitting alone? Flashbacks, muddle, nothing.

Now I'm here working in the bar. Before that it was Santiago apparently, then Jonno's, now here? Nearly at the end of the world, Finisterre. Then where? God help me.

What are facts without proof? I'm sure I've heard that somewhere. Questions, no answers.

Me, Shaun, Me, Ben. I need to clear my head.

'Just going for a walk, Maria, won't be long.'

✦

I've grown fond of this room; I feel safe for a start and being at the back of the house it's quiet; no-one bothers me. No-one interferes. Jonno's was a great place to stay, he's a fun guy but he put pressure on me to be sociable when I didn't want to. I know I reacted badly when he told me I'd have to move on but actually, if I'm honest I was ready for a change.

This bed's also a lot comfier than at his for a start, easy enough to sit on as the chair is ... well, it's seen better days. There's a nice vibe here just me and Maria with Carlos helping when necessary. Surprisingly, I'm getting stuck in where the barn is concerned, manual labour seems to suit me, I can lose myself in it.

These past couple of days have turned me inside out. Those grey eyes in the photo she left, they seem to bore into me. I can't deny they are so like mine?

All I know for certain is, I am me. What I don't know, who is me? I'm Shaun for God's sake, Jonno says so, Maria says so but Dai– Mum says I'm Ben, her son. The other guy, Patrick says I'm Ben, I'm a mate of his, apparently. The photo looks like a Ben which is the biggest confusion out 'cos it looks like me staring out at me. Is a Ben more clean-cut than a Shaun? Who's more likely to have dreadlocks? A Shaun or a Ben? I really don't know. I don't know anything. None of this makes sense and it's pissing me off.

Shame I don't have a photo of me now, come to think of it I don't seem to have anything except what I'm wearing at the moment and what's in my backpack, which is mainly stuff and clothes bought here in Spain, at least I suppose they were bought here – pants (one pair M&S) that's UK isn't it? And some unknown Spanish brand – local market probably. Rest of my possessions, let's have a look. Could be from anywhere ... 'made in Portugal', 'Made in Vietnam' ... hmm, no help there.

I like this part of the world, suits me. No pressure, but can I stay forever? I don't suppose many people pass this way in the winter. Jonno said most bars along this stretch close. Might need to go back to Santiago, or Burgos, there's bound to be work there but that's not going to solve the Daisy dilemma. The UK? That's where I'm meant to be heading, but why? I seem to have gone full circle. God, help me.

This guy Patrick's due here soon, he's gonna help with the barn. We're getting on well enough, I like him, he lets me take the lead, sort of waits for me to start talking. He acts like a regular guy, seems to know more about me than I do of him, at least I suppose it's true what he says. His past life sounds crap, can't have been much fun for him. Missing dad, alcoholic, absent mum, Gran did her bit by the sounds of it. Bit of a loner. No wonder we seem to get on.

The thing that's really confusing me, stressing me, is he also calls me Ben whilst Maria – and Jonno call me Shaun, which I am, aren't I? So why the two names? Where has Ben come from? Ben and Daisy, Mum and son, so they say. I don't know. What's Burgos got to do with all this? Is there any significance to the third person he mentioned? What happened? Something's getting at me. Patrick was there, told me he knew I had a scar on my leg. How did he know if he hadn't seen it? I was there, so the postcard says. Daisy wants to help me, but back in the UK. She's gonna get a temporary passport sorted. Patrick's hanging in here to keep me company, says he's got nothing better to do. Well, that's his story.

So, it's all down to me, I'm at the end of the world so can't go farther west. Patrick's going to stick like a limpet. Daisy's sorting the passport. I need to clear this cotton wool head. I seem to have a mum and I've got a dad and grandparents apparently. I feel like shit, my head's all over the place. I need to stop – somewhere. Find out who I really am. What happened? Something did. I can feel it.

Trouble is, what happens if ... if I don't like what I find out? Then what? Would I stay there? Wherever there is. Where do I belong? Patrick seems to think all will be well, he seems quite clear in his head about me and Daisy. Daisy? Mum? I really don't know what to think.

I guess if it all goes pear-shaped Jonno would let me come back, he'd let me doss down. So would Maria come to think of it, they've been good to me, I'm sure they'd take me in again. But ...

Does it come back to the need to know who I really am and what has happened?

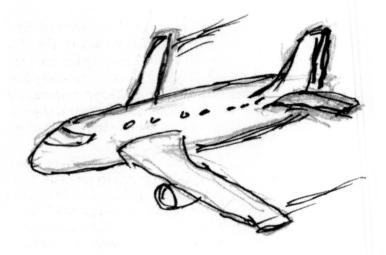

16

Journey's End

A FEW DAYS later, Patrick phoned to say Ben had agreed he would accompany him back to the UK. He didn't elaborate beyond admitting his concern around Ben's fluctuating state of mind and potentially losing any confidence that was being built between them. He explained he was keeping their conversation on a superficial level which seemed to flow best when they worked on the barn restoration.

I was over the moon, albeit initially felt a little disappointed Ben didn't himself phone but Mum reminded me that in his mind I probably was still Daisy, not his Mum. I had to accept we didn't know what was going on in his head, I didn't know how he saw himself but I could understand him questioning his own identity. From Patrick's conversation his intention seemed positive and the last thing we wanted to happen was for Ben to change his mind.

'One step at a time.' Mum's wise words became my mantra.

Dad mentioned the subject of Ben and his aim to raise money for the hospice that had cared for Sam in his last days. I felt guilty that I had forgotten but Mike stepped in and agreed to organise this, allowing us to concentrate on our aim to get Ben home.

There was so much to do and so much for Ben to assimilate and I was anxious for him and his mental state but I had to allow him to make his own decisions, live his hopefully last few days in Spain as he chose whilst we planned for his imminent return. Alongside that ran the risk he might disappear again unless we could arrange for the emergency passport quickly.

Dad found out how to obtain the necessary paperwork needed and was happy to travel to Spain. Shaun insisted on accompanying him promising he would keep a low profile. In the end, following hastily sought professional advice, it was agreed their sudden presence might trigger more buried memories to the detriment of what had been achieved so far. We therefore organised what was needed to be done and put our faith in Patrick who was happy to act on our behalf. Ben seemed to trust him … and so we await their return.

Glossary

Albergue	Basic hostel for Pilgrims
Bocadillo	Simple baguette using Spanish bread
Casa Rural	Rural tourist accommodation often an old farmhouse or homestead
Cerveza	Beer
Compestela	Certificate awarded on completion of the pilgrimage
Credential	Pilgrim passport stamped at each stage
Hostal	Simple lodging often with private bedroom offering food and drink
Hostel	Shared dormitories with basic washing facilities
Jambon	Ham
Meseta	Flat, open plains with steep climbs
Panaderia	Bakery
Parador	Luxury hotel often in a converted historic building- castle or monastery
Tortilla	Spanish omelette using eggs and potatoes